52
WAYS
········ TO ········
FEEL
GREAT
TODAY

Increase Your Vitality

Dr. David B. Biebel
James E. Dill, MD
AND
Bobbie Dill, RN

FLORIDA HOSPITAL
Since 1908

52

WAYS

TO

FEEL

GREAT

TODAY

52 WAYS TO FEEL GREAT TODAY

TO EXTEND *the* HEALTH *and* HEALING MINISTRY *of* CHRIST

PUBLISHER AND EDITOR-IN-CHIEF	Todd Chobotar
EXTERNAL PEER REVIEWERS	Linda Gill, RN, LPC, Bruce Incze, MDiv
INTERNAL PEER REVIEWERS	George Guthrie, MD, Bill Largo, MDiv
BUSINESS DEVELOPMENT	Stephanie Lind, MBA
PHOTOGRAPHER	Spencer Freeman
COPY EDITOR	Pamela Nordberg
PRODUCTION	Lillian Boyd
PROMOTION	Laurel Dominesey
DESIGN	Judy Johnson

PUBLISHER'S NOTE: This book is not intended to replace a one-on-one relationship with a qualified health care professional, but as a sharing of knowledge and information from the research and experience of the authors. You are advised and encouraged to consult with your health care professional in all matters relating to health. The publisher and authors disclaim any liability arising directly or indirectly from the use of this book.

AUTHOR'S NOTE: All stories in this book are true and used by permission. Most are disguised to protect the privacy of those involved. Stories may include composite characters.

Unless otherwise noted, all Scripture quotations are taken from the *Holy Bible, New International Version*. Copyright © 1984, International Bible Society. Scripture marked KJV is from the *King James Version* of the Bible. Scripture marked NASB is taken from the *New American Standard Version*, Copyright © 1977, the Lockman Foundation. All Scripture quotations used by permission. All rights reserved.

For volume discounts please contact special sales at:
HealthProducts@FLHosp.org | 407-303-1929

*Cataloging-in-Publication Data for this book
is available from the Library of Congress.
Printed in the United States of America.*

PR 14 13 12 11 10 9 8 7 6 5 4 3 2 1
ISBN-13: 978-0-9839881-2-0

For more Whole Person Health resources visit:
FloridaHospitalPublishing.com
Healthy100Churches.org
CreationHealth.com
Healthy100.org

Contents

Share with Us

WOULD YOU LIKE TO SHARE YOUR STORY OR idea with people around the world? Then we would like to hear from you.

First of all, we see this book as a *dialogue*, not a *monologue*. So we would love to hear what you think works well in this book and what might be improved. But we also want to hear your fresh new ideas! What things do you do on a regular basis to have a great day—especially things not already mentioned in this book?

Why? Because we would like to make this book into a series, and we're looking for more fun, creative ideas with true life stories to include in the next volume. Should we use your suggestion and story, we'll be sure to give you credit for helping us help others, and we'll even send you some free copies of the book in which your story appears when it's published.

If we can't fit your story or ideas into the next book, it may make its way into our newsletter or one of our future seminars. So if you would like to participate in this ongoing series with us by sharing your comments, suggestions, ideas, or personal anecdotes, here are three ways to reach us:

1. Go to our web site: FloridaHospitalPublishing.com and click on "Submit Your Story or Idea." Then follow the instructions for submitting your thoughts.

2. Send us an e-mail at Comments@FLHosp.org. Be sure to include information on how we can reach you so we can give you credit for your idea.

3. Visit us on Facebook and leave a message on our wall with your story or idea. Go to: Facebook.com/FloridaHospitalPublishing.

Thanks again for reading. Here's to your good health,

Todd Chobotar
Publisher and Editor-in-Chief
Florida Hospital Publishing

Dedication

T O THE MEMORY OF THE SWISS PHYSICIAN Dr. Paul Tournier, whose wisdom and works continue to inspire our commitment to Whole Person Health.

Acknowledgments

W E WISH TO THANK SUE FOSTER (MA, LMFT) for her invaluable contribution to our efforts to produce this book. She helped with the research, evaluated and proofed chapter drafts, and drafted numerous chapters herself. Her expertise in the fields of mental health and counseling was especially valuable whenever the topic of a specific chapter touched on those subjects, and her longtime interest in and involvement with music improved the overall harmony we were seeking. We also wish to acknowledge several contributions of personal stories by Bruce Incze, who retains the copyright on those stories. We thank Jeff Olson for his contribution to the chapter "Go Where the Wild Things Are," to which he retains the copyright, and for his encouragement and support, including his personal involvement with the events described in the chapter entitled "Be the Bear." The story by Mike Brooks in the chapter "Tune to the Maker's Channel" is copyrighted by the author and used by permission.

The Voice of This Book

W HEN WE SAY "WE" OR "OUR," IT MEANS THAT all three coauthors agree on the point in question. When one of us is describing our individual perspective or experience, we identify who is "speaking" in each case, by name.

Introduction

WOULDN'T YOU LOVE TO FEEL GREAT TODAY? Us too! That's why we wrote this book. In the pages ahead you'll discover fifty-two simple suggestions that could help you have a great day today and many more in the days to come. These suggestions are based not only on our own experience and observations, but many have solid scientific evidence to support their value in promoting your health and enhancing your happiness. We've been careful to identify which are supported by good research, and which depend more on the wisdom of the ages and may yet need modern science to catch up with their truth. We hope you'll give all these suggestions serious consideration and that you'll give many of them a try.

Of the hundreds of possible topics we might have chosen to include in this volume, we've focused on these particular suggestions because, taken together, they have significant value physically, emotionally, spiritually, or relationally. These are the four elements that we believe contribute most to healthier or happier living. At the same time, we realize that health or happiness cannot be scripted or nailed down, because they are better viewed as verbs than nouns—in other words, one's health or happiness is a dynamic total of one's relative wellness in all of these arenas at any point in time.

We also endorse the perspective on health that is presented in the "Creation Health" model developed by Florida Hospital, which uses the word "CREATION" as an acronym for elements of healthy living that have been shown to contribute to longevity—specifically, Choice, Rest, Environment, Activity, Trust, Interpersonal Relationships, Outlook, and Nutrition. In fact, *52 Ways to Feel Great Today* is one of the resources of the "Healthy 100" movement for individuals, companies, and churches. You can learn more about this movement in the back pages of this book and online at www.Healthy100.org. Specific connections with the CREATION acronym are listed in the appendix.

As we've created this text, we've kept in mind that readers vary in their approach to having a great day, and even in their expectation or definition of what such a day might entail. Some people are extroverts, so our suggestions regarding getting "out there" socially and interacting with life in other ways will seem like putting on a well-worn running suit. Others may be more introverted, preferring activities focused more on inner growth than on things that require physical conditioning or social interaction. Our hope is that whatever your personality, this book will build on your strengths while inviting you to try some new things from time-to-time.

Every suggestion in this book is supported by at least one true story showing how the practice or thought process in view has proven helpful to someone a lot like you. Yes, sometimes the stories are actually about us . . . the authors . . . but that's also because we're a lot like you. We've included these anecdotes because we wanted to encourage you to be as inventive, imaginative, playful, creative, or adventuresome as your personality will allow, knowing that what has worked for others might also help you improve your own life, day-by-day.

On the other hand, there aren't a lot of to-do lists, such as three ways to achieve this or that, or ten steps to a happier, healthier life. That's because we think that most such lists really miss the point that you are who you are, and in order to really become all you can become, you need freedom to live and move within the context of the way you, and only you, think and act. Our hope is that you will find enough flexibility in these "ways to have a great day" that you'll actually be able to find things that work best for you.

Our primary goal is to encourage you to respond authentically to the challenges of your own life as you know and experience it . . . and to always remember that you are made of very special stuff. Without a doubt, someone made that way should never be content with "good enough" when "great" is such a short stretch away. Reach for it!

Your fellow pilgrims,
Dave, Jim, and Bobbie

Foreword

W E HEAR A GREAT DEAL ABOUT INNOVATION IN business. We don't hear much about it regarding one's life. Disruptive innovations like the iPod, iPhone, or iPad emanate from core values like design and beauty. Steve Jobs said of design, "Most people think design is what something looks like, but the truth is design is actually how it works."

How does feeling unreasonably great work? It starts with *being* unreasonably great, which involves being a part of something bigger than yourself. For a long time I thought the biggest thing I could be part of was downhill skiing, the Olympics, and everything surrounding those. But since I retired from professional athletics, I've learned there is an even larger story in which we all have equally important roles.

Trust me. Be – Do – Have . . . is very different from Do – Have – Be. *52 Ways To Feel Great Today* is a quick reminder guide that *being* joy, happiness, and abundance are always at hand. It is a permission slip to *be great* amid fifty-two field trips that will help you *feel great*.

Everyone needs a wise, spiritual mentor. One of this book's authors, Dave Biebel, is mine. Everyone needs somebody who pulls you further into the light. I often push back. He challenges me to write a better story with my life. Dave's gift is his pen and it is built to last. In this book, Dave and his co-authors share a slice of heaven by showing us what it looks like with our feet on the ground. They write about good news through "how to" storytelling.

Ruminate upon these *52 Ways* and then author your own. If you do, your inner Tigger will find new joy day-by-day. Embody one each week and you will occur brighter in the world. Master just one, as a metaphor for *being* meaning, and you will be good news walking.

Jeff Olson
Two-time Olympian
Three-time USA Downhill Champion
Pan Am Games Gold Medalist
Business and Social Entrepreneur
Loving Husband and Very Proud Dad

1

Turn Pretzels Into Thanksgiving Dinners

To do more for the world than the world does for you—that is success.
                                                            – Henry Ford

TRY HELPING SOMEONE ELSE. THIS IS CALLED "altruism," and it not only benefits those you help but is a proven way to reduce your own stress and anxiety. Helping someone else is guaranteed to help you feel better about life in general, and it will get you involved in something that is bigger than yourself.

Scientists have studied the effect that helping others has on the human body. If you've ever helped someone, you've seen the benefits of your compassion in the joy on their faces. But what about your own health and well-being? That feeling you've probably felt after helping someone is called "helper's high," and it has been studied for its effects on physical and mental health and even longevity.

Stephen Post, PhD, a professor of bioethics at Case Western Reserve University School of Medicine in Cleveland, Ohio, has headed up several studies on altruism, benevolence, compassion, generosity, and kindness through the Institute for Research on Unlimited Love. The premise for his studies is that altruism can be an antidote for stress. This follows up an earlier study done by researchers at Cornell University involving married women with children. They assumed that the more children a mother had, the greater stress she would be under and, therefore, that she would die earlier than women with fewer children. After following these women for thirty years, however, they found that the number of children, education, class, and work status did not affect longevity. What did affect health and longevity was volunteering: "Fifty-two percent of those who did not volunteer had experienced a major illness compared with 36 percent of those who did volunteer." Other studies have shown that older adults who volunteer live longer than those who don't—a 44 percent reduction in early death.[1]

A volunteer chooses to serve a community or organization without getting paid. If you've done any volunteering you know the satisfaction that comes from doing something just for the love of doing it and helping others. If you are interested in doing some volunteer work, contact a nonprofit organization in your community and in your area of interest. Many communities also have organizations that list volunteering opportunities. Nonprofits are always looking for extra help and seldom have the funds available to pay for the needed staff. Volunteering is a good opportunity to rediscover your passions and really make a difference. The average amount of time people volunteer is around fifty hours a year—less than one hour per week. But even if you aren't able to make a commitment for an hour a week or a few hours per month, you can volunteer for a one-time event such as a community walk, a dinner, or some other kind of special event.

In addition to helping others through an organization, each

of us has nearly unlimited opportunities to make a difference, one person at a time. For example, have you ever taken a meal to someone who needed it, invited a single person to have dinner with your family, taken an elderly person shopping, mentored a troubled teen, or some other such act? If so, then you know the pleasure that helping can bring the helper as well as the one who is helped.

On a recent news report out of Nashville, Tennessee, a ten-year-old girl turned twenty dollars into enough money to provide two families with a Thanksgiving dinner. She won the money on a local radio station and spent that money to make chocolate-covered pretzels. She then sold those in the community and raised $150. She and her family delivered bags of groceries to the families in need, saying, "We want your family to have a good Thanksgiving like ours."

"I was really sad knowing that they couldn't have Thanksgiving like we always do," she explained during the newscast. So she decided to do something about the need that she recognized.[2]

Helping others can involve times of working together. Those who volunteer for Habitat for Humanity know the joy that comes from building a home for someone and then turning over the keys. Or perhaps you've taken a short-term missions trip with a group from your church and made a difference in another land. During a group effort, the gifts and talents of each individual combine to make the effort more effective. Young people who go on mission trips with their youth groups have reported that these times have drawn them closer to God and have given them a greater sense of his will for their lives. Many adults who do missionary work report that their vocation had its roots in the positive experiences they had on mission trips during their teenage years.

You may not have money to give, but you probably have time

and talents that are needed somewhere in your community or even somewhere else in the world. Sometimes helping another person is a spur-of-the-moment thing, and sometimes it takes planning. But in any case, it's hard to be depressed and negative when you know that you are doing something positive for a needy person, for a group, or for the world at large. Caring is the key. Helping is the result. If you feel down today, try looking for a way to make a difference, and then get out there and help somebody who needs it. In doing so, you'll be making life better for someone else, while at the same time making life better for yourself. It's one of those very rare win-win situations, for sure.

IF YOU WANT TO FEEL GREAT TODAY . . .

Do as the famous line says, "Give and it will be given to you." To experience a helper's high, give others a gift of your time, talents, or treasures. You will be rewarded in physical, emotional, and spiritual ways as you see the joy it brings to others. You'll also gain new relationships. So give of yourself and notice how compassion improves your health; as a result, you'll gain more than you give.

Make a Love Alphabet
— For Yourself

*Why are you trying so hard to fit in when you were born to
stand out?*
— Ian Wallace

E ACH MORNING WHEN SHE LOOKED IN THE
mirror, Misty struggled with inferiority feelings. I (Dave)
had the privilege of working with her during my time as
an editor of a Christian publication. Outwardly, she was attractive, capable, indeed very special, with exceptional skills as a
magazine designer. But she found it nearly impossible to see
herself as she really was.

Misty had grown up with everything she'd ever wanted, with
the exception of unconditional love. Her parents divorced when
she was nineteen, which more or less ensured that she would
never have any kind of reasonable relationship with them. The
next five years were dominated by Misty's search for love, which
she found partly through faith and partly through a relationship
with an older woman, Stacy, who became her surrogate mother
with a goal of filling in the vacuum in Misty's inner self.

Sometimes Stacy even tucked Misty into bed with words the young woman had never heard but will never forget: "Good night, love." Yet, tender as such love was, Misty hated herself for needing it. So Stacy's goal became to try to teach the younger woman how to nurture and sustain herself.

"Stacy helped me visualize a healing place, the place where I wanted to go," Misty said, "because I got so frustrated with how long my healing was taking. She could see the changes, but the increments were so small, I couldn't see them myself. In order to illustrate where I was headed, she read me that childhood story about the moonflower that blossoms at night. She told me I would know when I was healed, and she would know it too. And she promised to give me that story as a milestone when the day finally came. Shortly after I moved to Colorado, a package arrived from Stacy. It was the moonflower story, written out in longhand."

One of the most creative ways that Stacy helped Misty see and value her true self was through a "love alphabet" that she created for Misty. It was written out one letter at a time on the pages of a sticky note pad:

A: Misty is authentic. (Not phony)
B: Misty is beautiful. (Not only physically)
C: Misty is comforting. (Reaches out to hurting people)
D: Misty is deep. (She looks for more than superficial characteristics)
E: Misty is energetic. (Loads a fast dishwasher)
F: Misty is fervent. (Intensely devoted)
G: Misty is generous. (Gives out of love)
H: Misty is home-loving. (Loves the qualities of home)
I: Misty is insightful. (Sees with more than eyes)
J: Misty is just. (Sees fairness in all things)
K: Misty is kind. (Not mean)

L: Misty is lovable. (Easy to love)

M: Misty is a mother's delight. (I'm proud of her)

N: Misty is needed. (She's important to me)

O: Misty is outstanding. (No ordinary girl here!)

P: Misty is poised. (She handles different situations with aplomb)

Q: Misty is quality. (Knows good stuff and is good stuff)

R: Misty is responsible. (Always dependable)

S: Misty is spunky. (Spirited, plucky)

T: Misty is trustworthy. (She can be trusted to do it, keep it, say it)

U: Misty is understanding. (Perceptive, fine-tuned)

V: Misty is valued highly. (By many, mainly Stacy)

W: Misty is wonderful. (Amazing, remarkable, very fine)

X: Misty is X-tra. (Out of the ordinary)

Y: Misty says yes. (She is open to receive love from many)

Z: Misty has zest. (Keen pleasure in living and loving)[1]

Alfred Adler wrote: "To be a human being means to possess a feeling of inferiority which constantly presses towards its own conquest. The greater the feeling of inferiority that has been experienced, the more powerful is the urge for conquest and the more violent the emotional agitation."[2] And, we might add, the greater your need to be better than anyone else, the deeper your feeling of emptiness may become.

Most people have feelings of inferiority from time to time. If this feeling is pervasive, the result is often a fierce competition with others—the kind of competition that puts others down in order to elevate one's own self. This is why some people think they have to win at all cost, as is expressed by such statements as "Winning isn't everything—it's the only thing."

The net result is detrimental psychologically, sociologically, spiritually, and even physically. For example, some very remarkable young women, including Karen Carpenter, Ana Carolina Reston, Christy Henrich, and Heidi Guenther, starved themselves to death (anorexia nervosa) because they became obsessed with their weight's effect on their beauty or their performance as compared with others.

The drive to win at any cost can injure or destroy relationships. For example, one fellow we know was a fairly good athlete. But his need to fill his inferiority void was evident one night when, after a friendly game of softball, the wife of his longtime friend asked him why he had played so aggressively. "Because they are the enemy," he said without hesitation.

Spiritually, it's very easy to develop what is sometimes called a "worm" mentality, which can happen from being told that we are evil to the core and bring nothing to God by faith except our totally unworthy selves. People who are bombarded with this message can feel "lower than a worm." But if God loved you enough to send his own Son to pay the penalty of those sins on your behalf, can there be any doubt that he loves and values you more than you can imagine?

IF YOU WANT TO FEEL GREAT TODAY . . .

The next time you're looking in the mirror, instead of putting yourself down, why not say, out loud, "Here's looking at you kid . . . and remember you're: A=awfully . . . B=beautiful . . . C='cause you are so beautiful to me!" And then remind yourself that you're not just speaking for yourself, but you're speaking for the One who made you just the way you are.

3

Go Brain Jogging

Aging experts need to spread the word that cognitive decline is not an inevitable part of aging. Doing the properly designed cognitive activities can actually enhance abilities as you age.
                                                    – Elizabeth Zelinski, MD

IN TERMS OF YOUR BRAIN, YOU HAVE A CHOICE, for as that catchy phrase says: *Use it or lose it!* You have this choice every day. You can sink into a brain fog by doing something passive like watching TV, or you can take your brain jogging, which can be done anywhere, anytime, and it's free! In fact, many people consider exercising their brain just as important as exercising their body. Some of us have mentally challenging jobs that automatically exercise the brain. When critical thinking is necessary, or constantly changing skill sets are required on a daily basis, your brain will stay in tip-top shape.

But when the most challenging thing you do each day is decide which TV show to watch or what to cook for dinner, it is time to add brain jogging to your to-do list. If we are not exercising our brains, we are much more likely to become forgetful. Our dream of continuing to lead active and productive lives as we age depends in part on staying active mentally.

Doctors assure us that any brain-stimulating activity is better than nothing. We have an enormous amount of brain potential waiting to be tapped, and each time we learn something new, our brain power grows! It is never too late to work toward becoming the prodigy we were meant to be. Brain activity and learning keep us challenged and engaged in life, and that is healthy.

We have heard about the benefit of doing crossword puzzles, reading, and playing chess, but what other brain-jogging activities are recommended? We may find a wide range of suggestions coming from many directions. Ads will promise us that if we buy the latest computer-based "brain fitness" game, our memory will improve. These programs claim to improve the brain's speed in processing and recalling information, something we all would like to be able to do. Research is ongoing and will prove interesting when it is available. Knitting and typing have been shown to improve brain function, but only until we learn the activity well; then it loses its ability to challenge us. Frustratingly, once we have the patterns down, the long-term benefits disappear. Experts suggest that we wake up our brains by doing tasks like brushing our teeth or eating with our nondominant hand. Try showering or eating with your eyes closed. It is hard to do but engages a whole different set of neurons.

Any kind of creative "work" is known to improve brain function and perk up our day. Creative writing, painting, sculpting, and writing music all require the brain to lay down new pathways. Learning new dance steps or exercise routines has the same rewards. These are all like a mental 5K run. The ability to concentrate is a valuable skill, but unfortunately it can decline as we age. Studies are under way that hope to answer questions about the connection between brain exercises and thinking and concentration. Physicians know that as we age, we perceive the information gathered by our eyes and ears differently. This occurs because the information from our different senses often combines, making concentration harder.

Animal experiments conducted at Yale University and published in Behavioral Neuroscience showed that mental stimulation and enrichment started at any age significantly improved memory.[1] Adding physical exercise along with mental challenges in middle age seems to offer the greatest and most widespread benefits in memory function. This knowledge greatly encourages baby boomers who are determined to keep a sharp mind.

A research project at the University of Southern California is the largest study ever done on aging and cognitive training using a program available to the public. In this excellent study, 524 healthy adults, age sixty-five and older, were divided into two groups. One group participated in the Posit Science Brain Fitness Program, while the other group completed a traditional computer training program. The group involved in the Posit Fitness Program showed superior improvement in memory—a gain of about ten years. Participants noticed improvement in a number of areas, including everyday tasks like communication skills as well as remembering names and numbers.[2]

Dr. Stanley Karansky was a ninety-year-old retired physician who benefited greatly from the Posit Fitness Program. He told his personal story in Norman Doidge's book *The Brain That Changes Itself.* Dr. Karansky lived a full life as an anesthesiologist and finally retired at the age of seventy. But retirement was not for him, and he retrained himself and worked as a family physician for another ten years. Dr. Karansky became interested in the Posit Fitness Program after retiring for the second time and found the program to be sophisticated and entertaining. He claimed that he did not notice any differences in the first six weeks, but in week seven he began to feel more alert and less anxious, and his handwriting improved. He felt better about himself in general, and his wife reported that he was more responsive and engaged in talking to people. He loved board games and word puzzles as well as Sudoku. He noted that when he became interested in something, it quickly became a passion. He was able to concentrate completely on his subject, a skill that researchers say is necessary for plasticity changes to take place in the brain. His interest in astronomy led him to become an amateur astronomer, buying a telescope and learning all he could. He also delved into rock collecting, crawling about in ravines to gather specimens. At age eighty-one he studied about Antarctica and, fascinated, traveled to see it for himself "because it was there"![3]

We may not all be able to travel to Antarctica, but we can follow Dr. Karansky's lead and do some serious brain jogging every day so we can live life to the fullest.

IF YOU WANT TO FEEL GREAT TODAY . . .

Keep in mind that, as with the muscles you can see, "use it or lose it" also applies to your brain. So add "brain jogging" to your daily routine. Experiment until you find some brain-enhancing activities you really enjoy. If possible, get a "brain jogging" partner for added fun and accountability. The basic principle is that what is good for your heart is also good for your brain.

4

Count Something
Other Than Beans

Appreciation can make a day, even change a life. Your willingness to put it into words is all that is needed.

— *Margaret Cousins*

UNLESS YOU ARE LIVING SOMEWHERE THAT'S just been hit by a natural disaster, you really can have great hopes for your day if you look at your situation through an optimistic lens. We all need to learn to celebrate what is.

One early morning, a nurse we will call Ellen slouched into the hospital to start her six-thirty shift. She had been up with her twins on and off all night and was exhausted. The last place she wanted to be on this gray winter morning was the ER. She sent up a prayer for God to just get her through the day so she could go home and climb into bed early.

The ER was busy with the usual rounds of flu and accidents, and Ellen faithfully went through the motions—taking patients' histories and vital signs, putting patients into cubicles, alerting the doctor, and giving the medications and treatments ordered.

By ten o'clock the waiting area was jam-packed, and Ellen was dragging.

Then she saw them—an exhausted mom and her two children wedged in the corner between an accident victim and an inebriated older man. Compassion flooded Ellen as she led them from the waiting room. The young mother, dressed in shabby clothes, looked at Ellen with enormous, sad eyes. The little ones, coughing and sneezing, were miserable and whimpering.

Suddenly Ellen felt a surge of energy as the mom began to tell her story: "We were evicted from our apartment and have been homeless for two weeks. The little bit of money I had is used up, and I have been trying desperately to get into the shelter. I was told it was filled up but to keep trying. My husband died years ago, but I have been able to make ends meet until"—her voice wavered—"I lost my job at the mill." With tears welling up in her eyes she admitted, "I don't know where to turn, and I am so worried about my children."

Thankful that she could help, Ellen set about making calls to social services and alerting the doctor so she could initiate care for the children. Two hours later a temporary home had been found for the family, and they were on their way with antibiotics and a large dose of hope. As they hugged Ellen and left, she leaned against the wall, shaken to the core.

She saw herself in the eyes of that desperate mom and was flooded with gratitude for all the blessings in her own life. She went home that afternoon with renewed joy, looking forward to spending quality time in the comfort of her home with her twins. Ellen's day was totally changed, and she never forgot the lesson in appreciation she learned as she opened her eyes that morning to see the reality of her own situation.

You may not have an experience as dramatic as Ellen's, but if you stop "counting your beans" (focusing so much on deficit-related details that you miss the positives), you will realize that you are far better off than the many who are trapped in more challenging situations, struggling just to survive.

Make it your goal to celebrate the times when you have a sense of peace and joy, knowing there will be days when you, like Ellen, would rather just stay in bed and let the world take care of itself. On those days remember what Albert Schweitzer said: "In everyone's life, at some time or another, our inner fire goes out. It is then burst into flame by an encounter with another human being. We should all be thankful for those who rekindle the inner spirit."[1]

Researchers R. A. Emmons and M. E. McCullough found that grateful, optimistic people have more energy, feel more connected to the world, are more spiritually aware, and even have better functioning immune systems. People who are able to see the positive side of their own life tend to describe themselves as happier and more satisfied in general. This holds true regardless of the participants' age, health, or wealth.[2]

Let your own inner spirit be rekindled as you count your own blessings, let them fill you with joy and thankfulness, and then share that joy with others.

IF YOU WANT TO FEEL GREAT TODAY . . .

You can jump-start your day, before you get out of bed, by thinking of three blessings you enjoy and thanking the Provider for them. Then, during the day, try to view your quality of life through the optimistic lens of seeing "what is" versus "what might have been" or "what may be." At day's end, again express your gratitude to the One who is the source of every good and perfect gift. A day with gratitude for its "bookends" surely is a gift, after all.

5

Cook Up Love
in the Kitchen

Sixty-minute meals have no more work or steps than thirty-minute meals; they just take their own sweet time getting to the table. They are like a mellow friend you could watch movies with on the sofa in the rain—comforting and cozy.
— Rachael Ray

SOMETIMES JUST THINKING ABOUT "WHAT'S FOR dinner" can be a bother. Today we don't just worry about what we have in the pantry; we worry about what's in our food. PCBs or mercury can lurk in our fish, mad cow disease can taint our beef, E. coli or salmonella could put us in the hospital! Are eggs good for you or bad for you? What about cow's milk? How do you keep up with the flood of information?

Relax. Healthy eating doesn't require a degree in microbiology. And sharing a meal and great conversation brings friends and families together. In fact, we can rediscover the excitement and joy of creating a healthy meal. If you doubt this, just tune into one of Rachael Ray's cooking shows. We guarantee you will come away laughing and energized about cooking and creating!

She gears her show to twenty-something new cooks, but baby boomers can have fun and learn a whole lot, too.

Creating a healthy meal begins with using the freshest, most natural foods you can find. Over the past few years, a whole new food vocabulary has developed. You'll see terms like "free range," "natural," or "hormone free" on labels, but did you know these terms are not regulated by law? What about "organic" food? To help us know which foods really are organic, the U.S. Department of Agriculture (USDA) has created an organic seal. To earn this coveted seal, foods must be grown, harvested, and processed according to certain rules about the amount and type of herbicides, pesticides, hormones, and antibiotics that can be used. The Environmental Protection Agency (EPA) reports that truly organic foods will not have been treated with any synthetic pesticides, sewage sludge, bioengineering, or radiation. Of course organic foods are more expensive. So how important is it really to buy only organic?

A few years ago, researchers presented their findings at the Institute of Food Technologists annual meeting and expo. Several studies have shown that organic tomatoes have higher levels of vitamin C, and organic broccoli and berries may have higher levels of antioxidants than those conventionally grown.[1] More studies are in the works. But thus far, in general, scientific studies have not shown organic food to be significantly more nutritious than nonorganic food, even if it may be safer to consume. So if most organic food is beyond your budget, perhaps one way to try to provide your family the best of both worlds is to buy the following twelve fruits and vegetables organic when you can get them, because they have been found to have the most pesticides when grown conventionally: peaches, apples, sweet bell peppers, celery, nectarines, strawberries, cherries, pears, imported grapes, spinach, lettuce, and potatoes.[2]

One way to get fresher produce is at a local farmer's market, where you may be able to buy a fruit or vegetable you have never tried! How about choosing a feijoa or a camu camu or even a carambola? These delicious antioxidant powerhouses are available at certain times of the year depending on where you live. When Jim and Bobbie are on assignment in Hawaii, Bobbie loves to venture out into the markets. Row after row of fruits she has never seen before look like they should be used in a table centerpiece instead of eaten, because they are so beautiful.

The Hawaiian vendors are very happy to teach a willing patron about the wonders of the island's produce. The lychee is an extraordinary fruit that comes in clusters of rose-colored, soft, fluffy balls. After peeling the outside, you eat the tangy white center, getting a burst of amazing nutrition. Bobbie's favorite is the dragon fruit. This is a breathtakingly beautiful fruit about the size of an apple. It is a deep pink with lime green, pointy scallops all over it. She learned how to cut it down the middle and then scoop out the delicious inside, eating it as you would a tasty pudding. So much fun, and healthy too!

Bobbie and her sister have fond memories of visiting their grandparents in Philadelphia and catching the excitement as the "huckster" would make his way down the street in his trusty old farm truck, enticing all to come buy his fresh produce. From blocks away you could hear his singsong call: "Sweet corn picked this morning. . . . Get yer Jersey tomatoes, four fer a quarter. . . . Freshest green beans in the city!"

"Our grandmother, Idie, would fly down the back steps with us at her heels and purchase the makings of a great healthy meal," Bobbie says. "We grew up believing that that corn and those tomatoes were the best you could buy anywhere. Sitting down to Idie's dinner of fresh chicken, green beans, corn, and Jersey tomatoes, with strawberry shortcake for dessert, is such a strong memory, I can taste it. If you grew up in a time when meals were made from scratch, you'll have such memories, too."

Cooking can be a solitary or group activity. Some just love the company of a healthy pot of soup simmering on a snowy day, while others enjoy having the kids by their side as they pass on the family's secret lasagna recipe. Some couples enjoy creating their culinary delights together.

Even if you don't yet love to cook, give it a try anyway. Preparing a meal engages our creative side. No one would disagree that a salad right from the garden or a homemade apple pie are works of art! The sweet aromas can remind you of happy hours in the kitchen with someone you love and can give your day a positive focus as you look forward to giving the gift of a healthy meal to your friends or family.

IF YOU WANT TO FEEL GREAT TODAY . . .

Turn what some might see as an inconvenient chore into a fun family learning and bonding event by creating a healthy meal together. Cook from scratch whenever you can, using the freshest ingredients you can find in your own garden or at the store or farmers' market. If you're just a beginner cook, you can learn and be inspired by watching a good cooking show on TV or by asking a friend who loves to cook to teach you what he or she has learned through the years.

.... 6 ....

Color Your World

*Decorate your home. It gives the illusion that your life is
more interesting than it really is.* — Charles M. Schulz

W HILE THE THOUGHT OF INVESTING A LOT
of time and money in a large home improvement
project may seem overwhelming, a mini makeover
can give your life a little more sparkle and zest.

Psychologists and decorators tell us that our immediate surroundings often influence our moods. Living and working in the
midst of boring, impersonal surroundings or clutter creates
stress and affects the quality of our work. Drab colors can make
even a sunny summer day seem bleak. Many a beautiful craft
project originated with an inborn drive to beautify the four
walls. Even in ancient days, cave dwellers mixed paint from clay,
leaves, and flowers to brighten up their world!

Adding color continues to be the prominent factor in creating
a pleasing space. Researchers have been fascinated for many
years by studying connections between the most popular color
choices and how they affect our moods and everyday enjoyment. Studies have been done around the world and seem to

point to the fact that choosing colors is ultimately very personal. We need to trust our instincts to find the colors that make us feel happy and secure. For instance, in Japan and England, warm colors are preferred for the interior of rooms. However, in the U.S., most prefer pastels.[1] The bottom line is that you need to find the colors and designs that are right for you. Remember, one of the latest trends is breaking the decorating rules, which results in an explosion of fun!

I (Jim) warmly recall my mother's knack for decorating. Mom and Dad had lived their entire lives in the South until my father was transferred to Schenectady, New York, with General Electric—in the middle of winter! My sister and I were preschoolers, and Mom was feeling the strain of being confined during the long, snow-laden winter months. However, her creativity and talent flourished. Some of my earliest memories are of Mom, with art palette in hand, balanced precariously on a step stool or flitting to and fro around the downstairs recreation room, painting an amazing wall mural. A smile was always on her face as she coaxed the bleak four walls to life right before our very eyes.

And what did she paint? A ceiling-to-floor rendition of a graceful cruise ship leaving New York harbor, bound for faraway places. We marveled at the lifelike passengers strolling the decks, often resembling her unsuspecting friends or family. The ocean spray was so realistic we pretended we could take a swim at any moment. The New York skyline gave us a sense of wonder and awe of the big city. That winter held many surprises as we watched Mom's mural completely transform the downstairs.

News traveled fast, and everyone who heard about her masterpiece in motion would drop by to watch her progress, marveling at her skill. That winter she inspired many a homebound housewife to beautify her own environment. I was amazed to see her mural still gracing the walls of that Schenectady home sixty years later when we returned to visit the old neighborhood.

The present owners told us stories about how it continued to amaze and surprise unsuspecting visitors.

We are not suggesting that you take on such an ambitious makeover project, but each one of us can find something to improve. It can be as small as a kitchen drawer that has been an eyesore for years. An hour's time and some pretty shelf liner and a new divider can change it into something that you will enjoy opening! A flea market find can be painted in creative ways to add a sparkle of color to a dark corner. A cluster of favorite pictures will bring life and happiness into a room. Or you might seek out some wall decorations with religious themes to remind yourself and any visitors that however we may feel at the moment, the Creator is always greater than the creation, and we can find a sense of peace in that.

As we (Jim and Bobbie) travel about with our work, we often live in apartments with neutral decor. "We make these places our own," says Bobbie, "by quickly assembling our display of family photos. Recently, we have added our grandchildren's drawings and paintings to create a 'traveling art show' to liven up the walls. Colorful placemats and candles are also a favorite way to transform. We love nature, so seashells, pinecones, or an arrangement of unusual river stones will find their way into our living room or onto windowsills. Once we found a beautiful piece of driftwood that we could not bear to leave on the beach, so it became a unique centerpiece for our dining-room table. We have learned to have fun and bring color and nature right into our house wherever 'home' is at the time, because these remind us of a Creator who gave us such beautiful things to enjoy."

Filling your home or work space with a few treasures from enjoyable outings will bring a smile to your face as your eyes wander from the computer screen or the dishes in the sink or when your mind needs a break from thinking about what must be done next.

Working on a limited budget? There are many mini projects that cost pennies and can be completed in just an hour or two. Pick up a yard sale lamp for an uninteresting corner. Spray paint it to match your color scheme, and glue a unique fabric or braid on the lampshade to make a real eye-catcher. Find some graceful tree branches, spray paint them in your favorite color, and nest them in a container inside. Are your cabinet knobs making your kitchen look old and tired? Pick up new wooden ones and, again, get out the spray paint and rejuvenate. Stenciling can also transform a room. Animal lovers can stencil a parade of impish kittens above the kitchen counter, or flower lovers can stencil wildflowers across the bottom of boring curtains. One creative friend stenciled her bureau drawers to brighten up a bedroom. Let your imagination be your guide, and see how a colorless room can quickly turn into one that is bright and alive.

IF YOU WANT TO FEEL GREAT TODAY . . .

Remember that your soul is nurtured by your surroundings. So let your heart be your guide to what needs sprucing up. Move the furniture or grab the paintbrush and redecorate something for a fresh new look! Begin with a mini project—something you can finish in a matter of hours. The instant gratification and lingering satisfaction will spur you on to even bigger things, or it may just give you one more reason to feel great about your day.

········· **7** ·········

Get Out of That Rut!

The essence of pleasure is spontaneity.
– Germaine Greer, author

ONE OF THE BEST WAYS TO FEEL GREAT TODAY is to do something spontaneous. This could be any spur-of-the-moment, "wild hair" idea, such as chucking the housework and inviting over a friend for herbal tea and cookies when you haven't started making the cookies yet. Better yet, take that tea and cookies to a friend you haven't seen in a while. Drop in unannounced, and watch the surprise and delight on your friend's face. You'll probably want to do it more often.

Perhaps you've practiced moments of spontaneity. Perhaps it was a love note tucked into your husband's lunch before he rushed out the door or a note in your child's lunch on the day of a big exam telling her you love her, are praying for her, and are confident she will do well.

You might send an encouraging e-mail to someone you love or someone who is going through a hard time. Or how about purchasing a bouquet of flowers for yourself at the market just because you deserve it? Or take some flowers to a neighbor who is recovering from surgery. Her smile will brighten your day. You might treat yourself to lunch because you just can't choke down another peanut butter sandwich while the kids are at school. Moments of spontaneity like this can add sparkle to your day and make the day of those who are on the receiving end of your thoughtfulness.

One spontaneity killer is the sixteen-hour workday that too many face today. They work at home as hard as they do at work, bringing their work home because there isn't enough time to finish it on the job. The things that are supposed to save us time (electronic gadgets such as computers and cell phones) actually cause us to take time away from those things that should be most important to us—relationships.

A study conducted by Stanford University reported that "as Internet use grows, Americans report they spend less time with friends and family, shopping in stores, or watching television, and more time working for their employers at home—without cutting back on their hours in the office. The more hours people use the Internet, the less time they spend with real human beings. Social isolation is on the rise. E-mail is a way to stay in touch, but you can't share a coffee with somebody on an e-mail or give them a hug."[1] This study was somewhat prophetic, since a later study by Harris Interactive found that half the women surveyed would give up sex for two weeks rather than live without the Internet.[2]

We were created for community, and the Bible talks about its value. Hebrews 10:24–25 says that we are to "consider how we may spur one another on toward love and good deeds. Let us not give up meeting together . . . but let us encourage one another." The early church met in small groups in homes long before it started meeting together as a large group in a church building. There is value in being together and having fun outside of the formal gathering of church. A spur-of-the-moment lunch with a friend, a picnic at the park, a last-minute game night, or any other spontaneous, unplanned activity can add fun and joy to being part of a community.

If you are a planner and organizer, being spontaneous might feel flighty or frivolous. After all, you reason, there are people who depend on me. I can't just do something unproductive simply because I feel like it.

Perhaps you are a creature of habit and don't like surprises or changes to your routine. If so, acting spontaneously from time to time can help you become more relaxed and uninhibited and more resilient should adversity come your way. Being okay with having some unknowns in your day can force you to focus on what you really need to get done so you can finish whatever it is and go play. Spontaneity can also help you deal with stress. The better you can cope with unknown situations, the less stress you will accrue.

Sandy is a single mom with four teenagers and a busy, demanding job. Yet she has learned the art and value of being spontaneous. She is always ready for some fun and often calls a friend for coffee or a movie on the spur of the moment. If you're feeling down, Sandy is there for you with a phone call, a home-cooked meal, or an invitation just to talk. How does she do it?

"Life is too short," says Sandy. "If I didn't get out of my rut and hectic schedule, I'd go crazy. Yes, I do sometimes let the mundane, necessary things go. My house isn't always the cleanest, my paperwork isn't always caught up, but I need to allow time in my life for some fun and being with people. I figure the responsibilities aren't going anywhere and will be there when I get back. Being spontaneous sometimes helps me deal with the stress of life and take care of myself."

IF YOU WANT TO FEEL GREAT TODAY . . .

Here are some ways to get out of your rut:

• Draw boundaries. When you have deadlines to meet, get those things done first. Reward yourself with something fun after a job well done.

• Realize that a little can go a long way. We're not talking about shirking your responsibilities but adding some spice to your life once in a while. Start a hobby, call or visit a friend without setting it up ahead of time, and so on. No agenda; just enjoy each other's company.

• Pencil it in. While this seems to work against spontaneity, it can add a little control to it. Because it's part of your schedule, you can respond to another opportunity, "Sorry, but I already have other plans."

• Be extravagant with yourself from time to time. Have that double chocolate ice cream, lie on the couch and finish that novel, take a lawn chair outside and just lie there for an hour and watch the clouds go by.[3]

8

Rent a Puppy, Kitten, or Kid

The opposite of play is not . . . work . . . it is depression.
– Brian Sutton-Smith

ENGAGING OUR IMAGINATION IS AT THE HEART of play, but as we grow older, imagination can be pushed aside. It's hard to always be an adult. Thinking, talking, walking, acting, and reacting like an adult takes a lot of concentration and work, and it's not healthy. Everyone needs down time that requires nothing but to be lighthearted and to laugh, play, and have fun! How? All it takes is a puppy, kitten, or kid—or all three at once.

Bobbie remembers a walk she took with her then three-year-old granddaughter, Taylor. They had not gone far before Taylor discovered a big knothole in a tree. Bobbie stifled the urge to suggest they continue on. Instead, she waited to see what Taylor was going to do. The knothole suddenly took on all kinds of possibilities as Taylor reached into her pocket and pulled out her ever-present Weebles family. For the next half hour Nanna and granddaughter played in the shade of the tree. The knothole became a "house" with many busy people at work and play. Pieces of bark and pinecones became beds and tables. Rolled-up leaves were ice cream cones, and little stones were chairs. They played "house" together until Taylor spied a little rock wall she wanted to climb. And then they were off and running, winding their way around the neighborhood, discovering all kinds of fun things. They laughed and watched the ants busy at work, counted the stairs to the water fountain, felt the wind blowing strong around the corner, admired the colors of the leaves, and picked some dandelions for Mommy. Then they returned home with lots of stories to tell!

If you can't beg or borrow a child, you can usually "rent" a puppy. Pet owners are often happy to allow an animal lover the chance to enjoy their pet. As you begin frolicking with your new four-legged friend, you will be spirited away. Your troubles will melt as you enjoy the animal's antics. Puppies will quickly tire you out as you try to keep up with their racing about in piles of fallen leaves or jumping jubilantly through snowbanks. An old glove becomes a ferocious beast to be shaken about; a piece of rope facilitates a great tug-of-war. The happiest of all puppy games is "fetch my favorite toy." Or maybe this puppy prefers a Frisbee. Perhaps it is a warm spring day and there is water nearby. Most puppies will love to splash. And yes, you will get wet. Chasing squirrels is a puppy favorite too, and you will marvel at the dexterity and determination displayed in the game. We guarantee that if you focus on the puppy's fun, you will quickly forget your problems and share in that fun yourself. Lose the ball? Poor Frisbee toss? Your puppy companion doesn't care; you remain its hero to the very end. You will enjoy a degree of unconditional acceptance rarely found in the adult world.

Kittens can be just as engaging. Watching their acrobatic antics will have you laughing in no time. A ball of yarn or a kitten toy sends them dancing about, creating their own one-ring circus. If you really want organized chaos, try engaging a whole litter of kittens at once! They are so entertaining as they discover their world. You will run for your camera to capture these adorable imps as they tumble about at play.

Most animal shelters are appreciative when pet lovers are willing to take a new litter of kittens or puppies home for a few days of socialization. It is hard not to keep every one of them, but you will be guaranteed a wonderful experience. And what a great way to liven up a visit from your grandchildren while teaching them about the care and feeding of God's little creatures. Puppies, kittens, and kids just seem to go together naturally and are the perfect companions to engage your own inner child. Animal behavior specialists tell us that the first few months of our furry friends' lives are the prime time for them to learn important socialization skills which will often make them ideal pets for a lifetime. Just as important is exposing the young children in your life to pets so they can learn gentleness and proper care and feeding, encouraging them to become benevolent animal lovers.

If you are not in the mood for romping about, don't miss the benefits of just sitting with an animal, petting and talking to it. It has long been known that having a pet is good for our health. Petting a dog or cat has been shown to lower blood pressure and provide other health benefits through the soothing and relaxing effect of touch. A study from the State University of New York at Buffalo looked at a group of stockbrokers who were being treated with medication for high blood pressure. During the study, half of them had their blood pressure taken during stressful events with a dog or cat nearby. The other participants were measured without the presence of a pet. The group with the pets experienced 50 percent less increase in blood pressure during mental stress compared to those who were not in the presence of a pet. The results were so surprising that many of the stockbrokers without a pet went out and got one![1]

Be on the lookout for a child, puppy, or kitten to serve as your playtime shepherd. It will be well worth your effort, enhance your health, and make your day a great one as you venture for a while into the world of play.

IF YOU WANT TO FEEL GREAT TODAY . . .

Make these play thoughts a habit:

- Take time daily to be lighthearted and playful. Renew your heart, mind, and spirit by being a kid again whenever you can.

- Promise yourself to add more laughter and play to each day.

- Engage the help of a child, puppy, or kitten (or all three at once!) to revive your own playful inner child.

- Enjoy your play time and know it is enhancing your health. You will be energized and feel alive again. The weight of your cares will diminish, for who can really play and worry at the same time?

.... **9** ....

See God's Glory
in Every Place

Lord, make me see thy glory in every place.

– Michelangelo

A WELL-NOURISHED RELATIONSHIP WITH GOD is a foundation of good health and a component of every great day. Believers find strength and encouragement through prayer or meditation, reading Scripture or devotional writings, listening and singing to worship music, and even dancing. Many report that they are much freer to participate in the latter activity when alone, as they are less inhibited than when in a group setting.

Times of private spirituality involve our mind, will, and emotions—our souls—as we focus on the One who put us here. And following Michelangelo's lead, we can learn to see God's glory in every place—our homes, nature, our work, and any other area of life. We can also share such times with our families in the privacy of our own homes.

In Old Testament times, the people of Israel took seriously

the importance of teaching and leading their children in worship, and family leaders took the primary role in doing this. This made it possible for religious heritage to pass from parent to child down through the generations.

The early Christian church began in homes where the gospel story was told and retold, sometimes by such well-known figures as Paul, who preached his message "from house to house" (Acts 20:20).

With our fast-paced lifestyles, finding time for individual or family spirit-feeding is very difficult. On an individual level, many people find the early morning hours are best, as this time sets the tone for the rest of the day. This can be accomplished by setting the alarm for a time before the rest of the family is awake. Many report that as difficult as this sounds, they actually begin to relish that early morning time and find that after a month or so of doing this, it becomes a habit. Others report that a time right before bedtime works best for them as it helps push out the busyness of the day and helps them sleep better. If you have time alone during the day while the family is out of the home, put on some worship music and sing or dance along.

Family spiritual activities can include prayer before meals, in the morning before work and school, or at bedtime. Any time there is something of concern can easily become a time to stop and pray as a family. Children will feel important when they are included in praying for loved ones or other concerns. You might plan a weekly family night aimed at expressing your faith in creative ways such as skits or reenactments of favorite stories from Scripture. One of our friends described such a family fun time:

> A local church we attended hosts a costume party called "family fun night" as an alternative to Halloween. Several years ago, the theme that year was biblical characters. Impulsively I suggested "Jonah and the whale." We spent three days

sculpting the whale from cardboard, papier-mâché, and wood—then painted it blue. When it was done, the fish was thirteen feet long, five feet tall, and three feet wide—so we could get it out our front door. (I hesitate to think how big it might have become had we no horizontal limits—probably life-size.) The "whale" had a hinged tail that moved back and forth, with a stick inside to control the movement. The front half of the whale had no bottom, so Heather and Travis [two of the kids] propelled it by simply holding on to a waist-high pole inside the whale and walking. When Heather lifted the pole, the whale's head rose and the mouth opened wide—I had hinged it so that the lower jaw would rest on the floor by gravity. Big white teeth lined the opening. We had read somewhere that one of the reasons Jonah got the attention of the people of Nineveh was because he was bleached white by the stomach acids of the whale. So we bleached Travis's clothes and painted him white. We attached a lobster and some seaweed to his shoulder. When he stepped out of the whale's mouth, he, like the original Jonah, caught the attention of everyone. As I recall, they did not even take a vote in the contest—since our costume was, fins down, best by far. But that didn't matter. What mattered was that Travis and Heather had been on a three-day-long wild ride with Mr. Dad, whose childlike imagination had been unleashed.[1]

When you take on this kind of family project or even a smaller one, your relationship with God will be strengthened, relationships within the family will be reinforced, and the children will gain the sense that to live a life of faith can be fun. So if you have kids at home, brighten your day and theirs by planning a creative family activity related to faith.

However, even if you have no children at home, you can still feed your spirit. Sixty-two-year-old Laura describes how she does this:

With age comes the tendency to reflect—to look back through the years and examine relationships, rethink choices, relive the struggles and triumphs, long for the intimacy of family and friends who have moved on with their lives or left this earth altogether. With age also comes the stark reality of looking forward and realizing that the future may look more bleak than the past. When I look too long in either direction I can be easily overcome with sadness and a sense of loss. The best way for me to dispel these feelings is to focus on the here and now relationship that I have with my Lord by means of worship. While reading my Bible and praying are essential, they do not get me into God's presence to the same degree that worship does. In my life, worship is the essence of my relationship with God. When I worship him I become more aware of who I am and why I was placed on this earth. I become more aware of the basic joy of living rather than the cares and troubles that abound in daily life. Worries, relationships, and challenges all fall into proper perspective. When I worship, I move to a higher reality than this earthly existence and enter into the "peace that passes understanding." Worries become smaller and the mist of loneliness vaporizes. What a joy to have this simple way of moving back to reality.

IF YOU WANT TO FEEL GREAT TODAY . . .

Keep your spirit energized through regular worship in a group setting. Include family or friends and make it a shared spiritual activity. In private, spirit-boosting activities often require a quiet mind, peaceful surroundings, and even perhaps solitude to diminish distractions and enhance your Godward focus.

10

Discover Your Mode
of Expression

We all have the extraordinary coded within us waiting to be released.
— Jean Houston

A SURE WAY TO BRING SOME SUNSHINE INTO A drab day is to explore the arts. No training or experience is necessary! Each of us has a playful, creative artist inside just yearning to be invited out. Painting, crafts, and sculpting are not only fun and relaxing but also have the potential to bring a surprising surge of joy into your day.

Researchers assure us that creativity is universal and brings meaning and better quality of life to all cultures. Yoshi Iwasaki, a professor at Temple University, explored leisure activities in various cultures. He reports that while aboriginal tribes may not have an actual word in their language for expressive activities, they fill their days with expressive forms such as dance, music, sewing, crafts, storytelling, and painting. The study found that the benefits include stress release, enhanced self-esteem, group harmony, and even survival.[1]

Many communities encourage budding artists with group activities. Beautiful murals are painted on boring town walls, and corporations encourage expression in creative ways. Olin Corporation initiated a company-wide project encouraging children of employees to draw pictures with a Christmas or holiday theme, which the company then showcased as the covers for their holiday card mailing. One fun-filled family artistic event was recently sponsored by the Bank of Hawaii. "A steady stream of parents and small children meandered through the exhibits, watched the entertainment and tasted all things purple. It was part of the Bank of Hawaii Family Sunday called Ultra Violet. . . . Sheets of white paper covered the east-side walls surrounding the courtyard. Purple scribbles, pictures and doodles covered the paper . . . and as one of the volunteers attests, 'Children will draw whatever is in their minds. Drawing allows them to be so expressive.'"[2] Adults had fun too, creating rainbows using water, black paper, and a drop of clear nail polish!

Jim's sister, Betsy, is a professional artist and has this to say about exploring the arts: "Today I realized that it's been years since I created anything artistic that someone didn't pay me for. When your hobby becomes your profession, you still find personal satisfaction in the process, but the 'joy quotient' can change. Once I was intoxicated with the thrill of creating a cuddly 'monster' for a children's book, using my imagination to bring it to glowing life with technique and originality. My impetus was the high I got from the process. We all evolve in what we do with our time and resources and why we do it. Sometimes it is no longer enough to feel better ourselves; we want to pass it on . . . to teach others how to do what we have found . . . to build a bridge from what we did to what our students will do better if we share the joy and the how-to. The thrill then doubles with the knowledge that they will catch the vision and discover a new outlet. I may have a few cobwebs on my own easel at home, but," she adds with fervor, "teaching the arts is joy undiluted. And nothing makes me happier than looking out over my classroom and seeing the students lost in their creative zone."

We can use many different media, and it is fun to try them all. For instance, spend quality time with any kind of clay. Try air-dry clay, which dries to a hard finish. Or how about Play-Doh or cheap modeling clay that is reusable forever?

How about making free-form sculpture out of trash or recycled materials? Assemble mailing tubes, Styrofoam peanuts, ribbons, and cardboard. Use a glue gun or some super tacky glue to stick it all together. Don't even try to make it "look like something"; just make sure it doesn't topple over when you quit holding it. Take it outside, place it on a drop cloth or old shower curtain, and spray it with white paint. String some miniature white lights on it, prop it near your front door, and listen to the comments of your friends. They may see you in a whole new way!

Get inexpensive acrylic paints and paint whatever you like—abstracts, copies of Van Gogh's sunflowers, horses, flowers, or objects like mailboxes, birdhouses, rocks, or shells. Then spray your creation outdoors with polyurethane or low-odor clear shellac. And then hang up your painting! It will make you smile every time you see it.

Having trouble getting started? Ask a child to teach you to paint! Pull out an old roll of wrapping paper and some paints and entice your young "tutor" to show you what to do. We guarantee that without a moment's hesitation they will dip the brush in the paint and be off and running, caught up in the moment, creating as they go! Mixing colors? No problem. Doesn't look like any rabbit you ever saw? No problem. Running out of space? No problem! Then comes the fun part when, with a little coaxing, they will tell you the story of the picture! All of us can paint just for the fun of it as long as we absorb the mind-set of a child.

• •

If you are a neatnik and want to give the arts a try without making a mess, try no-muss, no-fuss painting. Go to http://artpad.art.com, click on "paint your own," and paint something electronically! Not sure how to start? Click on one of the samples and watch someone else paint. Or take a "tour" in the online Art Zone of the National Gallery of Art in Washington, D.C., at: www.nga.gov/kids/zone/zone.htm. You can manipulate art materials and learn a little art along the way.

Creativity is part of how we reflect what is called the "image of God" in ourselves. It just takes some experimentation to catch a glimpse of what the Creator has tucked away inside of you. The Bible is full of examples of the arts being used for the glory of God, who has created every one of us with unique talents and gifts. Once you discover your niche, you will get hours of joy from expressing your creative side and enhance the quality of life of those around you. And who knows what could happen? Many a beginner has, like Betsy, blossomed into a real professional who can go to work every day to do what they loved best as a child . . . and then double the joy by passing it on.

IF YOU WANT TO FEEL GREAT TODAY . . .

Awaken the creative artist inside you. Discover your mode of expression and release it through arts and crafts—and feel the joy and exhilaration of creation. Proactively explore your God-given creative side by taking lessons, or joining clubs or groups focused on a creative activity. Experiment with painting, sewing, cooking, writing . . . anything creative—and savor the joy you feel both in the process and what it produces.

11

Catch the Experience

Many men go fishing all of their lives without knowing that it is not fish they are after. — *Henry David Thoreau*

WHETHER ON A NEIGHBORHOOD LAKE, IN A beautiful mountain stream, or on a peaceful river, fishing has always been something to enjoy. From putting a worm on your hook and catching a rainbow trout to learning the art of fly-fishing, fishing offers many ways to escape the stress of this world and grab some relaxation. As the saying goes, "A bad day fishing is still better than a good day at work." Of course, if you adopt the perspective that the "catch" matters less than the experience itself, then you'll find it more or less impossible to *ever* have a "bad" day fishing. The physical, psychological, and spiritual benefits of spending time in the great outdoors cannot really be measured. And when you share the time with someone you care about, the benefits are enhanced that much more.

Sport fishing—with rod, line, and hook—has a long history. But "modern" advances such as the use of a reel to hold the line and line guides on the pole did not occur until the late seventeenth and early eighteenth centuries. Modern line development is much more recent, with nylon replacing horsehair as late as the 1930s. Materials used for fishing poles have also evolved from wood and bamboo to fiberglass and graphite. Methods of fishing and the choice of tackle used vary by fisherman and also according to the type and size of fish being sought. Fly-fishing, in which an imitation of a fly or a nymph (an immature insect) is used to catch unwary fish, has become more popular over the past few decades. Many fishermen who use this method tie their own flies, thus adding hours of enjoyment and anticipation to the actual fishing experience itself. Women are increasingly taking up the sport also, which has spawned the development of specialty equipment, clothing, clubs, and publications.

Fishing is sometimes used to help people with disabilities or illnesses. Project Healing Waters is a nonprofit organization that, with the help of volunteers, teaches disabled veterans the art of fly-fishing. From casting and fishing to tying the flies, Project Healing Waters knows and understands the benefits that fishing brings to people. On the Project Healing Waters web site, many people have written personal testimonials as to how fishing has helped them. One California veteran wrote, "It really raised my self-esteem, and it felt like I could do something, because lots of [the] time we're told we can't do anything because we've got a mental illness."[1]

One of our young adult friends, Steve, wrote, "I started fishing when I was very young with the help of my grandfather, who taught me that fishing isn't all about catching fish but being outside and enjoying the people you are with. The very first fish I caught was one of the most exciting times as a young child, and I still remember it vividly today. My grandfather and I were on a lake in the Sierra Nevada Mountains when he asked me to hold his fishing pole while he set mine up for me. Lo and behold I felt a slight tug on the line and then another and then another, and then my line went tight, and all of a sudden I was fighting a rainbow trout. (Unknown to me, before my grandfather asked me to hold his pole while he got mine ready, he had waited until a fish had taken his bait. He set the hook very carefully so I didn't see it and then handed the pole to me so that he could get mine ready. But, hey, I still caught a fish.)

"I have been fishing for more than twenty years now," Steve added, "and about six years ago I started learning the art of fly-fishing, which is one of the healthiest things anybody can do outdoors. It's not just the energy expended in wading a stream or about catching twenty-five fish or hanging 'a big one' up on my wall but about being outside and enjoying the beautiful surroundings God made. Not long ago, I was on a fishing trip with my father at the Frying Pan River in beautiful Basalt, Colorado. The river is surrounded by red canyons and cottonwood trees and green pines. The water was clear, the air was clean, and the slight breeze made me forget all the worries of the world and focus on just being alive for that very moment.

"Then the 'big one' hit, and I mean big. I yelled to my father across the river, 'This thing's huge,' as I fought the fish with all of my might. With both hands gripped tightly onto the fly rod, I tried my very best to keep it out of the rapids and bring it closer to my net (which by the way probably wouldn't have been big enough to fit the fish). The fish (which I named Earl) fought me tooth and nail and moved into the nearby rapids. As he did, I heard the taut of my leader and then a snap. Yes, he got away, and I could imagine him laughing as he swam away, saying, 'I'm big for a reason, buddy.' We had a great day, but it wasn't as much about hooking Earl and then having him get away as it was that I got to spend quality time with my father, not thinking of my mortgage or car payments but enjoying the beautiful surroundings I was in. That day was very freeing, peaceful, and serene, unlike most other days of my life."

You can go fishing just about anywhere there is water, from a local lake to an oceanfront destination. In a new place, a guide can get you to a good spot and teach you a little more about fishing gear and methods to use there. Check with your state's wildlife department. Its web site provides information on where and when to go fishing, along with good contacts at your chosen fishing destination. Local fishing shops are good sources since the people who work there can tell you what's biting and where to go. Depending on where you choose to fish, you might be able to catch several different species in one outing, so it's best to read up on the regulations in advance. In any case, remember, it's not all about catching fish. It's about enjoying the outdoors and the beauty that surrounds you . . . and about spending quiet time by yourself or quality time with those you love.

IF YOU WANT TO FEEL GREAT TODAY . . .

Go fishing. But remember that the catch matters far less than the experience itself. Very likely, someone you know is longing to go with you, just to spend the time with you. The physical, psychological, and spiritual benefits of spending time in the great outdoors cannot really be measured. And when you share the time with someone you care about, the benefits are enhanced that much more.

12

Try Airborne Ecotherapy

When you send it flying up there
all at once you're lighter than air.
You can dance on the breeze, over 'ouses and trees!
with your fist holding tight to the string of your kite.
— *"Let's Go Fly a Kite,"* from *Mary Poppins*

KITE FLYING HAS BECOME A POPULAR PASTIME the world over. Kites are beloved for their beauty and ability to lift our spirits, but creative minds have also harnessed their wind energy for a variety of uses. And as Mary Poppins knew, kite flying can make us feel great!

A UK report shows the benefit of getting outside and involved in an activity like flying kites. Ecotherapy is the new term used for outdoor activity in a green environment, which has been shown to reduce tension, boost self-esteem, and decrease feelings of depression. Kite flying has long been known to distract us from our worries and bring on a peaceful state of mind.

The kite is believed to have been invented in the fifth century BC by the Chinese philosophers Mozi and Lu Ban. Written records indicate kites being used for measuring distances, testing the wind, sending signals, decoration, and various military operations. The first recorded scientific use for kites was when Alexander Wilson of Scotland used a kite train (two or more kites flown from the same line) to take temperature readings at different altitudes. In June 1752 Ben Franklin and his son proved their theory that lightning was a natural phenomenon (electricity), not "the wrath of God," using a kite and key during a thunderstorm. The invention of the lightning rod was the scientific outcome of this father-son outing.

Jim had one kite-flying experience that will forever be remembered in his family. Attending a family wedding weekend on the shores of a beautiful lake seemed the perfect opportunity to introduce his little granddaughters to the joys of kite flying. The girls, ages four and ten months, watched gleefully as granddad skipped unceremoniously from dock to dock by the water's edge, trying valiantly to catch the breeze and launch the colorful kite. An hour later, having taken all the advice from the growing crowd of spectators, an exhilarated but spent granddad explained that "we will try again later." The girls were not disappointed in the least, thinking they had already watched a production outshining even Disney, with granddad as the star. The kite stunt was not videotaped but was passed down by oral tradition through some friends and family who cheered granddad on from the porch of the hotel. Thankfully, the next day the kite soared triumphantly into the cloudless sky as two little girls cheered.

If you've ever had the opportunity to attend a kite-flying festival, you know what a breathtaking experience it can be. While traveling up the Oregon coast, we (Bobbie and Jim) rounded a bend and were suddenly immersed in a sea of hundreds of colorful kites, airborne and sailing majestically above the white sandy beach and waves. For miles you could see the different varieties and sizes, mesmerizing the excited crowd of onlookers.

Of course we had to stop for a priceless afternoon of learning and celebrating this modern-day experience of kite flying. Many kites had been meticulously made by hand; others were built to specifications to enable them to perform mind-boggling aerial feats. One family we met had begun flying kites on weekends and ended up turning the hobby into a thriving family business which became the largest kite store on the Pacific coast!

Avid sportsmen have harnessed the power of the kite to create many ways to ride the wind. Some adventurers fly on kites behind power boats. Kite sandboarding, kite surfing, kite buggying, and kite snowboarding have become very popular. New techniques continue to emerge, including kite fishing and even (are you ready?) underwater kiting. One way or another, an hour or two riding the wind could energize your whole day!

Kite flying is not only about fun and adventure; the military has utilized the kite for serious tasks. During wartime, kites have been used for signaling and for delivering ammunition as they soared above the battlefield. Cameras were also attached to disguised kites and flown high above enemy installations to gather intelligence. Kites were even given the role of protectors as they flew above our Pacific coast as well as over London during the twentieth century.

Modern-day technology is harnessing the kite to generate power. The German company Sky Sails uses kites as a supplemental power source for cargo ships, reducing fuel consumption. This innovative system went into full production in 2008. Makani Power Company in California is investigating the use of high-altitude wind currents harnessed by kites to generate electricity!

In many parts of the world, kites are beloved and used as the main symbols of celebration, from flying a beautiful kite bearing the name of your newborn to hoisting up huge kite-balloons in the form of animals or birds as centerpieces in parades. In Korea, kites are often used to send up good wishes for friends and family. Many Japanese have become so consumed by kites that they have been labeled tako kishi, which means "kite crazy." In Greece, a kite-flying tradition commemorates the first day of Lent, called Clean Monday. In Bermuda, a traditional kite is flown on Easter to symbolize Jesus' ascent into heaven.

Everyone loves kites. You may enjoy simply taking a colorful kite to a beach or pasture on a windy day for the joy and freedom you feel as you allow your mind to soar with your kite as it dances in the wind. Frances Weaver says her life was transformed one day when she agreed to go with her friend to fly a kite. She had been suffering from depression, but on this memorable day, as she watched her kite soar in the wind, she felt a new lightness, and a sense of hope chased away the dark cloud of depression. From that day on she reentered life, and she eventually even wrote a book called *The Girls with the Grandmother Faces: A Celebration of Life's Potential for Those Over 55*. Surely "painting the sky" with a kite is good for your heart and soul.

IF YOU WANT TO FEEL GREAT TODAY . . .

Get creative and make your own kite. Make it a family project with your kids, or grandkids, if you want to multiply the fun. Study the fascinating history of kite flying and its impact on world events. Make this part of the family project also. Then, when it's ready . . . go fly that kite! And let your soul take flight. Let it "dance on the breeze, over 'ouses and trees!"

13

Loin Cloths and Clubs Not Required

Civilized life has altogether grown too tame, and if it is to be stable, must provide a harmless outlet for the impulses which our remote ancestors satisfied in hunting.
— *Bertrand Russell*

I N ANCIENT TIMES, ONE'S SKILLS IN HUNTING AND gathering contributed to the welfare and survival of the "clan." These days, most of us do not need to go out and bag a moose or gather nuts and berries in order to feed our families. Nor do we need the skins of animals to dress for success.

However, while traditional hunting and gathering skills are no longer necessary for survival, humans are still strongly wired with a need to hunt and gather. If we are deprived of the ability to partake in these primal activities, we can become depressed and feel unneeded by our "clan" without even knowing why we feel the way we do. Research reveals that our "feel-good" hormones are activated when we are involved in the challenge and thrill of hunting and gathering, and our opinion is that this is true even when we are hunting and gathering other kinds of "game."

Dopamine, the brain's pleasure chemical, is activated when we are engaged in a new, exciting activity. It rewards the brain when we engage in certain behaviors. Many of us know the thrill of attacking a difficult new golf course or decorating our first house or apartment. Recently, dopamine has also been found to interface between stress, pain, and emotions.[1] In other words, when we are feeling poorly, a release of dopamine makes us feel much better emotionally and physically, at least temporarily.

The act of hunting and foraging sends a powerful signal to every cell in our body that life is good and that it is a time for us to live and grow and connect. On the contrary, when we become sedentary, especially as we age, our bodies sense the change. Something is amiss. Exciting, stimulating work has given way to long days in front of the computer or TV. Fattening foods prepare us to go into a state of hibernation. Before we know it we are depressed, turned inward, not sleeping, and battling obesity.

Many of us already engage in hunting and gathering several times a week, even if we call the activity something else—like "shopping." I (Dave) love to cook, and that survival skill often takes me on an expedition to the grocery store. I try to find the best ingredients at the best prices available. Anticipation comes from thinking about the magnificent feast I will prepare for the "clan" after I get my "prize" home. It may not compare with the thrill that cavemen experienced when they bagged a woolly mammoth, but chasing down a sale is enjoyable in its own right. The word sale is the key here. It feels great to shop wisely and leave the store having saved 30 percent or more. There's a spiritual component, too, when you consider the question of stewardship of our resources.

Most women enjoy shopping and especially hunting for bargains. Finding that perfect dress or present for your sister's birthday can bring much joy into your day. Every year in Massachusetts, Filene's Basement has a bride's sale. You can see the anticipation on the face of each bride-to-be as they line up early in the morning, prepared to rush the door when the hunt begins. The level of intensity calls forth primal emotions as each one scurries up and down aisles looking for that perfect gown. And then there is the jubilation that comes with finding that gown at a bargain price. As Erma Bombeck said, "Shopping is . . . a contact sport like football. Women enjoy the scrimmage, the noisy crowds, the danger of being trampled to death, and the ecstasy of the purchase."[2]

Bobbie's aunt, Nancy, loves antiques. She sees the beauty in the patina of the wood and marvels at the handiwork of the early artists and the uniqueness of their pieces. Aunt Nancy says, "I became interested in antiques in the early 1990s and soon was hooked on hunting for treasures. A treasure doesn't necessarily have to cost a lot. It only must be old, rare, and intriguing. To be a true antiquer you must have a love and appreciation for vintage decor, jewelry, and furnishings. You also must know how to care for and preserve them. I love old linens. They demand a lot of loving care. Antiquing makes you forget all other problems, and you lose yourself in the moment. I don't think I will ever lose the thrill of the hunt. You can profit in so many ways by doing something you love."

Of course, using shopping as "self-medication" for negative emotions can become a problem, as with any pleasurable activity. It can and does get out of balance and can even become a true addiction. "Retail therapy," as it is sometimes called today, is shopping with the primary purpose of making yourself feel better or improving your mood. Normally a short-lived habit, it's often done during times of stress or depression. Items purchased during periods of retail therapy are sometimes called "comfort buys," and when put on your charge card, this is one quarry that can come back to bite you later. Jenny says, "I was a 'shop till I drop' kind of person. When the going got tough, I went shopping. I knew where to find anything you wanted, in which store, and for the best price. I used shopping to try to fill the empty hole inside and ran myself and my family into debt. It took counseling to help me see that I was addicted to shopping and to help me really learn to like myself without it. I still like to shop but now reserve it for the times that I need something or have the money to splurge on the one thing I've had my eye on for a while. Shopping has become a 'want to,' not a 'have to for all the wrong reasons.'"

So learn to use your instinct for hunting and gathering for the right reasons—to enhance your health and enrich your life. Enlisting friends and family in this endeavor doubles the fun. In Aunt Nancy's case, it opened up a new career that she shared with her husband "in retirement." Uncle Pete, although playfully protesting each time she came home with a new "find," loved the challenge of refinishing and giving those treasures a new life.

IF YOU WANT TO FEEL GREAT TODAY . . .

Satisfy your inner hunter and gatherer. Whether hunting for sales or gathering wild mushrooms, go wild with the exhilaration of the hunt. Some activities to try are: shopping for that bargain or perfect gift, finding a hidden treasure in "grandma's attic" or the local antique shop, or even hunting for, gathering, and then sharing "nuggets" of truth from wisdom literature or the Scriptures.

14

Get Wet

Row, row, row your boat gently down the stream,
Merrily, merrily, merrily, merrily, life is but a dream.
— Children's song, often sung as a round

HERE IS A "WATERTIGHT" WAY TO FEEL GREAT today. Gather your kids, friends, and family and head to your nearest water park. A water park is an amusement park that provides slides, chutes and ladders, water games, float rides, splash areas, and sun decks, often with most of the activities under cover. For a nominal fee you can escape for a day of barefoot fun for all ages.

The first water parks appeared in the 1940s but did not in any way resemble the spectacular parks emerging today. The water park industry has exploded; the U.S. now has about a thousand parks, to which more than eighty million people flock each year.

A visit to the water park is guaranteed to set your inner child free. It is reminiscent of those fun-filled days you spent at the river, ocean, or lake. The exhilaration and relaxation you will experience can't help but brighten your mood. Researchers assure us that swimming and water activities enhance our overall health. An hour or so in the water can benefit our circulation, flexibility, endurance, and posture. Water play will also meet our recreational and social needs and is sure to bring all the health benefits of laughter.

My (Bobbie's) first experience at a water park was definitely a mood-changing event. We had just flown across several time zones to visit our son and six-year-old granddaughter. She was excited about taking us to the water park for the afternoon, and we were hoping it would free us from a case of jet lag! We entered the mammoth, heated, sunny "bubble" and were amazed at the array of activities surrounding us. Beach music played, and kids and adults were having the time of their lives frolicking around in the ankle-deep splash pads and lagoons. I was immediately thankful to discover that the water was pleasantly warm, and lifeguards could be seen everywhere instructing and helping.

Our granddaughter sensed the "lazy river" would be the place to start, so we climbed into a gigantic inner tube and floated along with the winding river current, laughing and talking. Suddenly we were drenched as a huge wooden bucket emptied its contents on those of us coming around the bend! Okay. Now I was alert to the obstacles and was in the game. After the lazy river, it was time to tackle the giant slide. We grabbed an inner tube raft and started up the winding staircase, discussing if we should take the medium-sized slide or the really big one. "Oh, let's start with the medium-sized one," I begged. "Okay, Nanna, but then you will want to try the big one too," she assured me as we started up the stairs. I was jubilant to see the lifeguards giving careful instructions to riders as they climbed aboard their inner tubes. Before I knew it we were nested in, and with the flash of the green light we went swirling our way down the long tube, laughing and yelling the whole way, finally splashing into the lagoon at the bottom.

"Come on, Nanna, let's do it again!" And so we did, eight more times, agreeing we were having fun on "our slide" and didn't want to do the one that was twice as big or the one that thrusted you down in the pitch dark! Next it was time to head to the big lagoon, where I was looking forward to a respite, but no—instead our creative six-year-old envisioned us as the wild ponies of Chincoteague swimming across to the island. We had such a wonderful time that I find myself, as I am writing this, already looking forward to our next trip.

Water parks are definitely a way to stay young at heart while also getting some great exercise. For those looking for a bit of relaxation, most parks offer comfortable recliners on an indoor sun deck, reminiscent of a day at the beach. Many have lagoons complete with gentle waterfalls and, of course, a lazy river. The sunlight just by itself is healthy and uplifting, especially in the dead of winter. Water parks are a great place to overcome a fear of the water or teach your youngsters to swim.

Even if you decide just to bask in the sun on the sun deck, you will be entertained as you watch the "three-ring circus" below you. Warm water has a calming effect on the body, and as long as you can adjust to the continuous lively music played throughout the park, you can come away feeling like you had a minivacation. One attendant, a senior citizen who volunteers twice a week, related that she would not trade the experience for anything and was convinced that the warm water and humid environment were even helping her arthritis.

If your idea of a water park is a hose and piece of plastic on a backyard hill, you will be amazed at the new millennium versions of water park themes. The largest indoor water park in America is the Water Park of America in Minnesota, which covers 70,000 square feet and contains a ten-story-tall slide and chutes complex. At some other large water parks you can zoom down a seventy-foot drop with your friends or family tucked into a raft called the "family bowl" or have a water fight on the deck of Captain Hook's boat. You can ride in an aerial swing equipped with a water cannon and gleefully spray passersby in the lagoon below, a perfect antidote for the "blues." Most parks have a family raft ride navigating exhilarating special effects. In one park you can snorkel in a huge saltwater reef stocked with tropical fish. Many water parks include a wave pool with surf-sized breakers.

If you are interested in trying out the water park experience, go to http://www.waterparks.com to find one near you. Gather a group of friends or family and prepare for a great time, or even consider making a water park an invigorating place where you could volunteer and have some fun for free!

IF YOU WANT TO FEEL GREAT TODAY . . .

Don't be "wet behind the ears," get wet all over. Find some water and splash your way into a new day. Go to a water park—or hit the beach, splash in a puddle, run through a sprinkler . . . because when you get wet, you get fun. Expect the exercise and exhilaration to enhance your health and make memories. Get wet with your kids, or if you don't have kids, get wet with somebody else's kids! Watching the children have a blast will put a smile on your day!

15

Better Than an Antidepressant

The YMCA has always been committed to fitness and healthy lifestyles.   *– Jim Robinson*

A WHOLE VILLAGE AWAITS YOU AT THE LOCAL YMCA. Walk inside and you'll see women playing a rousing game of basketball, dads swimming with their kids, teens inline skating, preschoolers happily painting pictures, moms in a Bible study, or a group of adults attending a health seminar. The Young Men's Christian Association was begun in London in 1844 by George Williams to replace life on the streets with Bible study and prayer. It quickly grew into an international Christian oasis to strengthen families and communities. Now in the new millennium, with concern about the rising epidemic of unhealthy kids and adults, YMCAs are reinventing themselves as community centers with an emphasis on holistic health. New programs are being added that provide a wide range of activities for people of all ages who want to improve their health. The genius of the Y's programs is that they are committed to helping people pursue well-being in mind, body, spirit, and relationships. This mission ensures that you will be surrounded with opportunities guaranteed to improve not only your day today but also your quality of life in general.

Choose from a host of invigorating programs. You can join a basketball, soccer, or baseball team. Join a social club or learn to dance. Volunteer in any number of community groups. Join a support group or outdoor adventure group. You can even join an aquatic program for water aerobics or scuba lessons. Each community has special opportunities that reflect its unique geographical area. In all areas emphasis is placed on caring, honesty, respect, and building strong families. Participating is a great way to meet new friends with interests similar to yours.

All 2,686 of the YMCAs in the United States are committed to addressing our unprecedented health crisis by serving people of all ages, races, faiths, backgrounds, abilities, and income levels. As of April 2009, the U.S. YMCA had 20,916,698 members. Of these, 10,426,328 were men and 10,490,370 were women. In addition, kids ages seventeen and under numbered 9,422,524. YMCAs are accessible to almost everyone; 64 million households live within three miles of a YMCA. In addition, this nonprofit organization is one of the largest volunteer powerhouses in the world, serving more than 45 million people.[1]

Pat Murphy, age sixty-six, joined the Personal Fitness Program (PFP) at her local YMCA. "The staff is so cheerful, friendly and helpful," she said. "When I walk through the doors into the bright light, hear all the sounds and feel the energy . . . I know I'm in a special place and I leave all the worries and stress behind." Pat lost twenty-one pounds during her twelve weeks in PFP; she emerged from the program with more energy, strength, and flexibility and is still shooting for more endurance and stamina and to drop ten more pounds. One of Pat's big payoff moments happened after being at the Y for only twelve weeks, when a friend commented, "Pat, you are looking great. You are absolutely vanishing!"[2]

Fifty-two-year-old Rob Beno says, "The YMCA is a place to meet new friends and an affordable place to exercise." Rob started exercising in 2005, and he shows determination, persistence, perseverance, and patience. He enjoys exercising in the downtown location because it is just one block from where he lives, and he never has to wait to use the machines. "Exercise makes me feel better, both physically and mentally," says Rob. Marcia, Rob's personal trainer, has been a role model and an inspiration. "She pushes me to do better and has always been there to answer questions," Rob says.

As a result of the program and support, Rob dropped twenty-two pounds. He keeps his meals down to about 500 calories each and makes time in his busy life to actually go to the Y, "suit up," and exercise! Rob wants to share with the world how exercise makes him feel. As someone who suffers from clinical depression, his mood is improved after his exercise. "I really feel on top of the world for a few moments. A lot better than my antidepressant makes me feel," reports Rob.[3]

So for a natural high, get to the "Y."

IF YOU WANT TO FEEL GREAT TODAY . . .

Visit your local "Y." Whether your goal is to lose weight, increase strength, get healthy, have fun, or make new friends . . . your local YMCA is close by to help you achieve your goal. You will experience improved physical, emotional, spiritual, and relational health as a result.

16

Delight in the Elements

Measure your health by your sympathy with morning and spring.
                                            – Henry David Thoreau

IN DAYS GONE BY, MANY HOMES, SCHOOLS, AND workplaces had a coveted patch of green where we could routinely escape and recharge. We could breathe fresh air, stretch and walk around, and gaze at flowers and trees or maybe even a distant mountain or lake.

At lunchtime, we would take our sandwich and head outside for a stroll and some laughter with our kids or co-workers. We felt refreshed and could return to the day's tasks with renewed energy and perspective. Unfortunately, this practice has given way to the "working lunch," keeping workers inside at their desks.

Experts warn that separating ourselves from nature increases stress, and research has shown that immersing ourselves in nature not only is soothing but also protects our psychological well-being. Dr. Mardie Townsend is conducting the "Living High but Healthy" project in Australia to show how important it is for those living and working in the city to have exposure to nature. A host of studies report that immersing ourselves in nature can boost our immunity and productivity as well as increase our ability to deal with the day-to-day challenges of our lives. Having little or no exposure to nature has been linked with depression.[1]

Sue, a surgical nurse, had given birth to a longed-for son and quit the job she loved to stay at home with her baby. Simultaneously her husband, Jack, was drafted into the military as an Army doctor during the Vietnam War. Within a short time, Sue and her husband were relocated to an isolated Army base far from their friends and family. At first Sue was excited about their new life and set about making their tiny house a home, relishing every moment with their newborn son. Then the rainy season came. Sue woke to gray skies and teeming rain day after day after day. At first she busied herself with craft projects and taking endless pictures of her son's new milestones, but as time went on she felt more and more trapped and isolated. Always an outdoors person, she longed for even one sunny day back in her home state, hiking with her old friends. Her husband was very supportive but exhausted after his busy days at the hospital, and he looked forward to quiet evenings and weekends at home. Crushing guilt was beginning to overwhelm Sue. She knew how fortunate she was to have a beautiful, healthy baby boy and a loving husband who had not been sent overseas like so many others. Each day she would longingly look out the window for signs of life and a break in the constant downpour.

One morning she was overjoyed to see a neighbor with a young child bravely facing the elements. She had on a bright red slicker and had bundled up her six-month-old and perched her in a child backpack carrier. A large golf umbrella covered mom and daughter as she jogged across the lawn, tossing a ball for their black Lab, who was happily prancing by their side. Sue was transformed that day and set free to get back into the outdoor life she loved, her fears of taking her new baby out in the downpour banished by the other mother's example of going outside to play! It didn't take Sue long to don her rain gear and make a new friend as they took the first of many walks through the beautiful park with their laughing babies.

In the past few years, employers have become more aware of the benefit to their employees when they are given a few minutes of down time in a place with a tranquil view. Tables on a deck and an attractive, safe outdoor place to walk during lunch breaks can increase the satisfaction and productivity of an entire organization. Blue Cross and Blue Shield sponsors periodic lunchtime walks for working people around the country, hoping to promote more active, nature-filled lunch breaks. Groups of friends are encouraged to give it a try, and with a bottle of water and a protein bar, they are escorted around the block several times by enthusiastic trainers hoping to convince them to begin this healthy habit. Participants are often surprised to see how much more invigorated and relaxed they feel upon returning to their desks.

Hospitals, too, are finally placing importance on the healing properties of exposure to nature. Old, depressing, dimly lit hospital quarters are giving way to earth-colored walls, nature-inspired art, huge sunlit windows, and healing gardens. The most wondrous example of this that we (Bobbie and Jim) have ever seen in our travels is at one small community hospital in Lebanon, Oregon. A generous gift from an enlightened former patient enabled the hospital to create an elaborate healing garden in the center courtyard of the hospital. The exquisite ornamental trees and flowers and the pond laden with water lilies could be seen from every vantage point. Walking the hospital halls was a journey into nature as the garden was viewed through expansive windows embedded with an occasional stained glass creation depicting soothing Scripture verses. Patients and staff alike spent as much time as possible enjoying the benefits of this place of serenity. At one end of the garden a gentle waterfall cascades over colorful rocks and plants alongside the little "porch" where cancer patients receive their chemotherapy. As the benefactor knew it would, healing flourishes in this little Garden of Eden, for without a doubt, if there is any place on earth that our healing Creator loves, it is a garden.

Be proactive about immersing yourself in the beauty of nature. Celebrate the seasons and the weather. Make the most of your outdoor surroundings. Visit a stream, a forest glen, a mountain trail, a beach path, a bird sanctuary, a hill, or a garden. Study the flowers and trees, listen to the birds singing, notice the shades of color in the autumn meadow or sparkling lake or the hues painting the autumn leaves. Drink in the fragrant aroma of the woods or garden or the pungent, salty scent of the ocean breeze. Touch the velvety texture of the moss or flower petal. Feel the rain on your face or catch a snowflake on your tongue. Immerse yourself in nature. It soothes the soul, clears the mind, and guarantees you a great day!

IF YOU WANT TO FEEL GREAT TODAY . . .

Rather than complain about the weather, learn to relish it, whatever it is at the moment. Delight in the elements and you will discover a great secret—being in nature guarantees restoration. "It's elementary, my dear Watson." Concentrate on the sights, sounds, and fragrances, and soon you'll become a nature "word artist."

17

To Increase Your Energy, Test Your Skill

Live daringly, boldly, fearlessly. Taste the relish to be found in competition—in having put forth the best within you.

– Henry J. Kaiser

COMPETITION TAPS INTO OUR BASIC HUMAN desire to be a winner. Some of us are more competitive than others, but we all are energized when we test our skills against others. It's one way to enter into the fun no matter what our age, stature, or situation. We love to hear stories of courageous contestants who enter a competition with little chance of winning and walk away with the prize. Competition enhances our overall health and, if novelty is added, sparks our brain.

Scientists have been doing research on the importance of challenge, novelty, and invention to the ability of the brain to learn better. Neurobiologists have discovered that a novel environment enhances exploration and learning, but they have wondered how important novelty is by itself. A 2006 study was done in which participants viewed unique images while undergoing MRI scans. The "novelty center" (SN/VTA) of the brain—the area that spurs the brain to explore—was activated, showing the importance of novelty as opposed to some other types of stimuli.[1]

Bruce, a friend of ours, will never forget "The Great Race" staged one summer on the little island off the Maine coast where he spent summers as a boy. He told us:

> We never suffered from boredom, but sometimes we needed to be a little inventive in creating our own entertainment. To appreciate this story there is something you should know about my mother. In a word . . . short. In two words . . . very short. While she seemed to keep up with four boys and two dogs on our family hikes, I never knew her to go out of her way to exercise. Being boys, we were always running around the island, negotiating the craggy, rocky shoreline and climbing trees. One summer afternoon Mom casually made the statement that she could make it around the island in a certain amount of time that seemed rather preposterous to us boys. We howled with incredulity and laughter. That's how challenges get cemented in my family! Before anyone knew what was happening, the parameters of "The Great Race" were set. Mom had to run around the island in the prescribed time. She would start in front of the cabin, which is on the East Beach. She would then run around the island in a clockwise manner to where four laughing boys would greet her with a boisterous "I told you so," and a loving husband would console her. From high up in the horse chestnut tree one of us would monitor her run, while the other three would be lookouts, catching glimpses of her at different points. Pretty thorough coverage of the event added to the entertainment.
>
> Mom, with a twinkle in her eye, stepped into her slip-on island shoes and, without a thought to athletic gear to buoy her performance, announced she was ready! Three . . . two . . . one . . . GO! "The Great Race" was on. She made a sporty

start with the weight of representing all womanhood on her shoulders. We four boys probably made a few snide remarks—children are like that when parents are trying to prove something. As I recall, Mike was the announcer from the highest point in the tree; Danny and Steve were on the ground with the official timepiece, a wind-up Big Ben alarm clock. Mom made surprisingly good time down East Beach and then, like [she was] an Apollo space capsule passing the moon, we lost contact as she headed down South Beach. But we knew when we saw her again on West Beach we should have our first evidence of her failure. The time was being faithfully called out every thirty seconds. Mike had a clear view of the southwest corner of the island, and when she passed the elm tree she would be halfway done. But with half the time expired there was still no sighting of Mom. Thirty more seconds, and still no Mom. Another thirty seconds, still no Mom. "Wait, I see her," Mike yelled. "She's up by the eel grass." This was way past the elm tree! Instead of running on rocks, where she would have been seen rounding the elm tree, Mom had run on the sand below tide level. This meant a longer run, but faster and safer. It was the perfect strategy for her. Even from his perch high up in the tree, Mike was not [able] to see her again until she rounded the northwest corner. "Mom ho!" A quick check of the Big Ben alarm clock, and it was clear that Mom would lose the bet. We boys started gloating and laughing—a bad strategy for us. Mom heard us, and instead of quitting in exhaustion, as she later confided she was about to do, she reached deep for that last bit of energy and with seconds to spare, accelerated across North Beach and turned the corner in victory! Her glory was a little hard to take. And lunch that day didn't taste so good: bologna sandwiches with garnish of crow.

A great memory was made that day, and the story is guaranteed to be retold for generations! This is the subtle cement from which enduring relationships are made.

So try introducing some novelty into your competition, have some fun, and spur on your brain. It could be a race of sorts or a competition to build the best snowman or sandcastle. Stage a jump rope contest for the neighborhood kids, or how about seeing who can rake the biggest pile of leaves in the fall? If you have young enough children, you might even create a competition related to Bible characters as a way of getting a little deeper into your shared faith. For example, how about a "David vs. Goliath" competition, or a "Samson" competition to see who is strongest, or a "Nimrod" competition to find out who is the best shot with a bow and arrow (in Genesis 10:9, Nimrod is described as "a mighty hunter before the Lord"). Competitions could also include hunting for the best sale or hunting for the biggest collection of bugs from the backyard, for example.

The bottom line is that whatever competition you invent not only will make a memory but also could really improve your day.

Fun and wholesome competing elicits thrilling feelings and can create lasting and fun memories you will talk about often. And . . . when you make up the game yourself, the challenge and novelty enhance healthful activity in your brain.

IF YOU WANT TO FEEL GREAT TODAY . . .

Try creating a friendly competition, one in which everyone really is a winner. Fun and wholesome competition elicits thrilling feelings and can create lasting and fun memories you will talk about often. And . . . when you make up the game yourself, the challenge and novelty enhance healthful activity in your brain.

18

Find Out Why the Pen is Mightier Than the Fog

To keep a journal is to know the present is still under consideration, merely a first draft of your experience.
– Alexandra Johnson

A STRESSFUL EVENT, UNKIND WORDS, OR SCARY aches and pains can quickly rob us of our peace. We mull over what we should do or what we should say, mentally exploring in detail all the potential negative outcomes. When we find ourselves swimming about in all these feelings, one path to freedom can be found through writing. Journaling can transform your day. It untangles your emotions and helps you gain perspective and sometimes even find solutions.

Numerous studies have reported health benefits when we take up a pen and unburden our souls. Journaling can bring back our sense of well-being and improve our sleep and concentration. It has been found to lower blood pressure and heart rate, boost the immune system, decrease pain, and ease symptoms associated with asthma and rheumatoid arthritis. The research of Dr. James

Pennebaker has shown that "short term, focused writing can have a beneficial effect on everyone from those dealing with a terminal illness to victims of violent crime to college students facing first year transitions."[1] He found that it is not necessarily important to journal for a long time or even every day. Once every three or four days is often enough to bring relief.

Journaling may be one of the easiest of all "cures" to chase away the blues. Putting thoughts and feelings on paper is a form of catharsis, unburdening our hearts and minds. There is no right or wrong way to journal. You can choose to write in a beautifully bound blank book or use a legal pad or spiral notebook as your invisible listener. You can write whatever is on your mind, ignoring punctuation, spelling, and neatness! As you write about sadness, anger, frustration, or grief, you will eventually begin to feel calmer, gain insights, and feel more empowered. As the pressure of the newly exposed emotion begins to recede, solutions may emerge that you never thought of before. You may begin to see another's point of view, or the jumble of recent life events may begin to make more sense. The fog begins to lift as you see positive steps you can take to solve problems you are facing.

I (Bobbie) found solace in journaling after my mother's death. Mom was a marvel; she had a gift for enjoying life and went about living each day to the fullest. At age eighty-one she was still healthy, vibrant, and active as she spread joy around her corner of the world. Her cancer diagnosis was a shock to all of us, and we helplessly watched her quickly go downhill over the course of only a few months. Hope began to give way to acceptance as all the treatments failed. We surrounded her with our love and one by one said our good-byes. God was merciful, and my mother died peacefully at home in the circle of our love. I knew she was safely tucked into heaven, but the aftermath for us was deeply painful. Talking helped, but it wasn't until I turned to my journal that peace and joy began to return to my life. I wrote an "altar of words for mom" about her special qualities and our family times together, highlighting her great sense of humor and her wisdom. And I wrote about the empty place in my heart and the longing for just one more hour with her. God comforted me in a special way as I poured out my grief, and slowly I did begin to heal. I still miss her enormously and will still return occasionally to my writings to leave one more scrap of memory or tribute for me and for my grandchildren who never had time to really know her. My prayer is that she will come alive in their hearts someday as they read the stories about their great-grandmother.

Pauline relates, "I love to journal as a way to enliven my communication with God. I will read a passage of Scripture and then write a prayer back to God about the insights and thoughts that emerge from reading the living Word. Writing 'postcards to God' about life events helps me to keep a proper prospective and makes it easier for me to leave my worries in his capable hands. I have found that after a difficult challenge has passed, I can look back and see how God not only prepared me in advance but was with me every step of the way."

Many people, especially seniors, enjoy reflecting and writing about memories of days gone by. They find it therapeutic to immortalize certain events and people who made a major impact upon who they have become. These memories become a treasure for future generations and give the journaler satisfaction in knowing their special era of family history has been recorded.

Other uses for your journal might be to keep track of special dreams you have had or to record how an event changed your life. Cancer survivors often speak about the soothing effects of writing as they share their illness and recovery journey. It is also beneficial to record our blessings each day. These can be small events, like a beautiful sunrise, or something major like a family member returning from Iraq. Being thankful even for small things has a cascading effect upon our body, mind, and relationships.

You can become a word artist and journal about the exquisite things you see every day in your world. Take time to really study the colors and designs of the flowers, the graceful lines of the tree branches, the way the light skips through the water, the smile on the new baby's face. You can jot down snippets of uplifting conversations, drink in the different fragrances in your corner of the world, or maybe describe the taste sensations enjoyed during a special meal. Every journal is unique and a treasure to the writer, and perhaps it will also be a treasure to loved ones someday. Try it. Just pick up a pen and start journaling your journey.

IF YOU WANT TO FEEL GREAT TODAY . . .

Imagine you are the lead character in a unique and marvelous story, which you are discovering as you go. We're speaking of your life, of course, which is part of a larger story in which all of us have a part. Journaling can focus your vision for the future by helping you recall important snippets from the chapters already written. In the process, research suggests that your sleep will be improved, your immune system strengthened, and your sense of pain will be decreased.

19

Spell "Surprise!" in a Whole New Way

What greater thing is there for two human souls than to feel they are joined . . . to strengthen each other, to be at one with each other in silent unspeakable memories.

– George Eliot

WHEN YOU'VE HAD A CHALLENGING FEW months in your family life, you and your spouse may be left feeling a little discouraged and disconnected. The added stress has drained your energy. You wonder where the spark has gone as you plod through your separate responsibilities each day. If you can relate to this scenario, it may be time to try a proven way to jump-start your relationship: kidnap your spouse! If you are like most of us, just thinking about this crazy idea can engage your playful, creative side, and anticipating your spouse's reaction will make you laugh out loud every time it comes to mind.

We all know how important it is to bring spontaneity and fun into marriage. Research continues to investigate what kinds of things result in healthy marriages. A recent brief concluded, "It is not necessarily the sheer amount of time together, but the quality of the interaction as well that contributes to healthy marriage. In addition, it is not the specific types of things that couples do together that matter, but rather the fact that couples have positive interactions and enjoy their time together. . . . In addition to communicating and interacting, feelings of trust, caring, and love, as well as physical affection, represent important dimensions of a healthy marriage."[1] Yes, a surprise getaway could be just the prescription needed to enhance all of these elements!

I (Jim) first heard about this idea from a doctor friend who had come back to work after "kidnapping" his wife. His humorous story encouraged all of us at the lunch table as we vowed to give it a try too! Lou and his wife, Diane, who was just finishing her residency, had been on a whirlwind of busy call schedules and long, exhausting days. They had barely had time to exchange a few words each day, and those usually centered around finances or what to do about the family dog's new annoying habits. Lou had been thinking about how much they needed a weekend getaway but knew his wife would probably say, "No, now is not a good time! Let's wait until . . . ." But Lou knew in his heart that they needed some time together now. So he made a weekend reservation at a ski resort near their home, got a neighbor to keep their dog, secretly packed some clothes, and gleefully plotted Diane's Friday kidnapping. He just roared in laughter as he described the look of absolute shock, and then delight, on her face as he scooped her up in the parking lot as she was headed for her own car. Hearing Lou's tale was all I needed in order to start planning Bobbie's kidnapping!

I knew instinctively where we should go, having seen some ads for cabins in the woods on a mountaintop with a gorgeous view of the valley below. Knowing Bobbie's love for hiking, I made sure they had plenty of mountain trails. The cabins were

• •

sparse, but I knew all Bobbie would really care about was having a deck and a "real" wood-burning fireplace—her weakness! Perfect! I changed my call schedule and made a two-day reservation for the first weekend in October, two weeks away. I congratulated myself and started making a list of what I had to do to pull this off.

I realized immediately that our situation was much more complicated than my friend Lou's. Instead of one little dog, we had three children, two dogs, and a cat! So I made several calls and swore our friends to secrecy as they agreed to help with this grand scheme. I started slowly packing away things we would need for the secret weekend but ran into some snags as Bobbie would say, "Where in the world is my red sweater?" or, "I know I put my hiking boots by the door downstairs!" As the time grew shorter, I was almost giddy with anticipation. The day finally came, and as planned, my "accomplices" took over with the kids and our animals, promising a good time would be had by all. I had packed the car the night before, after Bobbie was asleep. Finally, on Friday afternoon, I went to pick her up when her shift was finished. I had a fresh drink waiting, our favorite CD playing, and a huge smile on my face. As Bobbie sank into the front seat, she started chatting about needing to hurry home because one of the boys had a game. Then I sprung it on her. She was speechless and then a little horrified, saying, "Oh, honey, we can't possibly go this weekend!" She anxiously started rattling off all the reasons one by one.

"Who will feed the animals?"

"The kids have all kinds of activities this weekend."

"I have a ton of wash to do."

"We are going to have the first frost and the plants have to be brought inside" (I had already taken care of this).

Then she turned and looked at me with an enormous smile and just started laughing. Success! And so began one of the most memorable getaways of our lives. We relaxed by the fire, hiked through the beautiful fall foliage, read aloud to each other, slept in, listened to relaxing music, cooked our favorite meals, and remembered who we were and why we had fallen in love. We had "church before our laughing fire" as we thanked our Creator God for our marriage and the beauty of the mountain. We were renewed in every way and went back home Sunday afternoon full of joy and hope. We were ready once again to pour our lives into our children from a full cup!

It worked so well that I began to recommend "kidnapping" to some of my patients who were suffering from overload syndrome. I have never had even one person come back to tell me it was a mistake. Through the years, Bobbie and I have continued to surprise one another on occasion. As we developed the "art of kidnapping," we discovered that, when a whole weekend is impossible, a few hours will do. An afternoon drive in the country, taking sunset pictures, a few hours canoeing, sledding after a snow, or dinner and a movie all add adventure and fun to the marriage. The surprise element makes it so much fun, and it can be done on a shoestring. Expanding the art of kidnapping to one of your children or grandchildren or to a good friend, a parent, or a sibling is also a lot of fun and builds wonderful memories.

We were so happy one day when we got a phone call from one of our grown sons telling us he was planning to "kidnap his grandmother" on her eighty-eighth birthday! He knew what she loved and had rented a convertible for a surprise drive around the countryside and made reservations at an authentic Italian restaurant. She had often entertained us with her stories about the days when she and her husband owned a convertible as newlyweds, as well as tales about the adventures she and her friend had studying art in Italy as young college girls. This surprise escape would be so uniquely tailored for her! As you can imagine, she was just thrilled and treasured the memory of that magical night with her grandson all throughout her remaining years.

So think about kidnapping someone you love, but be careful. Kidnapping can become a habit as you bring surprise and joy into the lives of those you love and experience how the planning and sleuthing can turn ordinary days into great ones.

IF YOU WANT TO FEEL GREAT TODAY . . .

The next time you need a getaway, make it a friendly kidnapping! It will be a love crime that will be cherished forever. Just planning the event will give you hours of fun, and sharing the intrigue can enhance communication, trust, caring, and affection. And sharing the story later or hearing your "victim" share the story later, with friends and family, will further enhance a great memory.

20

Think of How Strong You're Gonna Be

Don't think about how weak you are—think of how strong you're gonna be.   *– Michelle (Berry) Dougherty*

L IFTING WEIGHTS MAY NOT BE THE FIRST THING you think of when you want to feel great. After all, the memory of the last time you worked out in the yard too vigorously still lingers. But lifting weights may be a fast track to not only feeling better in general but also building self-confidence, decreasing pain from arthritis, warding off diabetes, and lowering blood pressure. It will most definitely make you feel better!

According to Dr. Nalin Singh, a physician and geriatrician at Royal Prince Alfred Hospital in Sydney, Australia, weight lifting should even be considered as a treatment for depression. His study of thirty-two participants over the age of seventy with a history of depression showed a significant reduction in depression levels in those who lifted weights during the study. Interestingly, twenty-six months after the study, 33 percent of those who had experienced a reduction in their depression through lifting weights were still lifting.[1]

A sixty-eight-year-old gentleman we will call Alex began to experience early morning depression and also to feel a little unsteady on his feet for the first time in his life. His wife noticed he had slowed down on the stairs and was even having trouble lifting his two-year-old grandson. Alex's physician could find no clues as to the reason behind this. Alex had not fallen, but he felt like his strength was waning. His physician suggested he get out more with people and work with a trainer at the YMCA to try some strengthening exercises. Alex was lean but not strong, and as he aged he had done less and less to maintain muscle strength.

Without realizing it, Alex had become quite sedentary, and this was taking a toll on his mental and emotional state. Alex reluctantly went ahead with his physician's recommendation and began working with an excellent trainer who took a real interest in him. The trainer designed a program of weight lifting especially for Alex. As Alex faithfully worked out in the gym three days a week, he quickly began to feel like a new person. Not only had he met new friends, but he was amazed at how quickly the exercises increased his strength and confidence. In addition to increasing his strength, Alex developed a much-improved posture.

After the age of sixty, many people begin to stoop a bit, jutting out their chin as they walk. This sets up a lifetime of handicaps and can lead to falls and broken bones. Alex learned the importance of strengthening his core muscles, the ones that keep our body in good alignment as we go about our day. Poor posture is a challenge to correct, so the sooner we start working on this, the better. "Core work" involves strengthening the abdominal and back muscles specifically and really cannot be done effectively without a knowledgeable instructor. Unfortunately, some have even been injured as they tried to do it on their own. It may look easy, but trust us, there are many important subtleties you cannot afford to miss!

Ben, age sixty, was an active fellow who loved to bike but had noticed he was having trouble with balance. After a fall, he checked with his doctor, who shocked him by saying that as we age the neurotransmitters in our brain in charge of balance start to deteriorate. This can cause us to trip or take a tumble because even mere walking requires a series of thousands of tiny adjustments to keep us upright. Ben was relieved to find that lifting weights actually repairs these important circuits. He ran, not walked, to the nearest gym and began a weight-lifting program which solved his balance problems! Ben was on the road to a happier, healthier life.

Cindy, on the other hand, had a different concern as she entered her fifties—belly fat. She had been fairly active and able to maintain a slim figure until, seemingly overnight, she noticed that padding around the middle. Cindy was familiar with the dangers of extra abdominal fat, especially in postmenopausal women. This "middle-age spread" can affect posture and, worse yet, has been linked to heart disease and other chronic conditions. Instead of panicking, Cindy did some investigating and discovered that lifting weights for an hour twice a week has been shown to control the unwelcome fat accumulation. She was relieved to know there was something she could do to turn this around other than to take up some strenuous sport that didn't interest her. She learned that a pound of fat burns only about five calories a day, but a pound of muscle burns about sixty. Encouraged, she took the next step and added some aerobic exercise and a healthier diet.

Over the last few years, imaging techniques have been used to test the effectiveness of different exercises on the muscle groups. Some of the old standbys were quickly changed as trainers learned to modify body movements to better target the necessary muscles. Researchers were surprised to actually see the impact that small changes could make on effectively working the four muscle groups in the abdomen, for instance. Some of the biggest changes were made in the techniques used to strengthen the body's core. Trainers call this "finding neutral spine" or "posture." Neutral posture involves aligning the body properly to minimize stress on joints, muscles, tissue, and the vertebrae. It eventually becomes a habit and allows a person to go through the day performing activities more comfortably, powerfully, and safely.

For many people, the thought of walking into a gym dressed in workout garb to face a lineup of foreign machines or a stack of shiny weights is beyond intimidating. This is why having a mentor by your side can help you know how to set goals and get started safely. Weight lifting is a science; injuries have occurred when people have tried to learn on their own. The National Strength and Conditioning Association is a good source for finding a qualified trainer in your area. Steer clear of trying to learn from friends, books, and videos at the beginning. You will do best with someone to tailor your training to your own individual body needs and quirks, whatever they may be.

IF YOU WANT TO FEEL GREAT TODAY . . .

Strength training increases your physical and mental agility . . . and your strength and confidence. It is great for everyone. If you don't have any weights to lift, lift your arm. Great . . . now . . . again while you count to ten! Just think of how strong you're going to be in body, mind, and spirit.

········· **21** ·········

Give Until You Feel Great

Instead of the old slogan, "Give until it hurts," it seems we
should say "Give until you feel great."
— *Douglas M. Lawson, PhD*

I T SEEMS IMPOSSIBLE THAT ANYONE IN AMERICA,
perhaps in the whole world, can have escaped the impact
of the recent economic crisis. Perhaps you or a loved one
or close friend has lost employment, a home, or retirement
funds due to a company's failure or experienced one of a wide
range of other potential losses, one of the greatest of which is
the sense of optimism and financial security that has been part
of our American mentality for a few decades now. "Shop till you
drop" no longer has the entertaining ring it once had for some.
These days, it's more like "Try not to drop while you shop, shop,
shop for something you can afford."

Most likely, you worry to some degree every day about your
finances. And those concerns get you down, perhaps way down.
You worry about how you'll pay the bills. You worry about
whether you'll be able to keep your home and car. You wonder
how you'll feed or clothe your family properly. And you pray

that no one for whom you have responsibility will become seriously ill, because there are zero funds at your disposal to cover even the deductible, if you are fortunate enough to have health insurance. Perhaps you worry that next week's pay envelope will include a pink slip, since, like so many, you live within one paycheck of financial disaster.

Here's a simple prescription to tap spiritual wealth even if your pocketbook is not as full as it once was and you're possibly feeling more than a little discouraged or anxious about it: give. You might even consider giving as much as a therapy session might cost, because giving is its own kind of therapy.

Give and you'll receive a blessing—if not financial, at the very least a sense of satisfaction and joy, for Jesus made it clear: "Give, and it will be given to you. A good measure, pressed down, shaken together and running over, will be poured into your lap. For with the measure you use, it will be measured to you" (Luke 6:38). The Bible has more to say about giving than just about any other topic, and with good reason—it's good for us.

Science is just catching up to this principle. In the past few years, numerous studies have found multiple health benefits from giving. In fact, the article "The Science of Good Deeds" by Jeanie Lerche Davis mentions fifty scientific studies funded through The Institute for Research on Unlimited Love, headed by Stephen G. Post, PhD, a professor of bioethics at Case Western Reserve University School of Medicine.[1]

In his book *Give to Live*, Douglas M. Lawson, PhD, provides the following list of positive benefits of giving:

Physical Benefits
- Greater longevity
- Significant reduction in toxic stress chemicals in the body (and so less stress)
- Enhanced functioning of the immune system

- Decreased metabolic rate
- Improved cardiovascular circulation
- Healthier sleep
- Help in maintaining good health

Emotional Benefits
- Increased self-acceptance
- Reduced self-absorption and sense of isolation
- Increased endorphin release (which provides a natural emotional "high")
- Expanded sense of control over one's life and circumstances
- Increased ability to cope with crises
- Stronger feelings of personal satisfaction
- Improved concentration and enjoyment of experiences
- Enhanced compassion, empathy, sensitivity to others
- Reduced inner stress and conflict

Spiritual Benefits
- Greater connectedness to God
- More receptivity to spiritual guidance
- Added involvement in charitable activity
- Heightened sense of appreciation and acceptance of others
- Sustained peace of mind
- Greater clarity about the meaning and purpose of life
- Enhanced quality of life[2]

There are many ways to give, of course. These include giving money or goods to individuals or religious or charitable organizations, volunteering time and energy to support a charitable organization, giving time to befriend a younger person who needs guidance (for example, via the Boys and Girls Clubs of

America), visiting people in nursing homes and other similar facilities, helping a disabled person cope with life's demands, using special skills that you may have to help others (for example, cleaning gutters for an elderly couple or helping a new widow organize her affairs and file her taxes), shopping for someone who can't get out, helping a struggling young mother pay her bill at the cash register, or sending a missionary a personal gift at Christmas. The possibilities are unlimited, because people with needs greater than ours are all around us.

"I had just quit my job at a prestigious university because of stress-related issues," Michelle said. "I was pretty sure I could get another job at the same university, but I didn't know when that might happen. I had some savings but wasn't sure how long that would last if I didn't get a job right away. About this time, I found out that a friend was in need of a rather large amount of money to pay her rent and to carry her through until she was paid from her new job. I was praying for her one morning when I felt prompted by the Holy Spirit to write her a check for that amount. I will admit that because of my financial situation, I was a little hesitant and somewhat scared. However, I've learned to listen when God says to do something because I know there is a good reason and that I can trust him to take care of me. I felt a sense of peace and knew that it was the right thing to do. That afternoon I stopped by her house and gave her the check. When I saw the joy and gratitude on her face, that was further confirmation that I had done what I had been asked to do. Within two weeks I had a new job at the university which is much less stressful and a better fit for me. Also, I had been having problems with my heating system. I had mentioned this to a friend out of state. Two days later, she sent me a check for the amount I needed to put in a new heating system. This has been further confirmation to me that when God says to do something, it's important to do as he says."

It is as Winston Churchill said: "We make a living by what we get. We make a life by what we give."

IF YOU WANT TO FEEL GREAT TODAY . . .

Remember that it is better to give than to receive because God uses a bigger shovel than you do. As you give, more comes back to you. And this applies not only to financial gifts—you can give of your time, your energy, your talent, your expertise, your love . . . just about anything that someone else may need, with the knowledge and confidence that in his own good time, the Lord will repay your generosity in full, with some left over. Not only so, it's therapeutic to give, even when it hurts (or we think we can't afford to do without what we're thinking of giving). For in giving we are reminded that we are blessed enough to have something left to give, when so many in our world today live in such difficult circumstances.

22

Hit Rewind

You never know when you're making a memory.
– Rickie Lee Jones

THE OLDER WE GET, THE MORE WE SEEM TO long for the "good old days" when life seemed simpler, anyway. We all get nostalgic from time to time, remembering those good times with family and friends, far-off places we visited, and fun events we participated in. Have you noticed, however, that small details about those times seem to get fuzzier as we age, and when comparing those memories with others who shared them, the details you all remember are somehow different?

Creating new memories every day for yourself and those you love and finding special ways of recording those memories helps keep them alive for years to come. This is especially important on those days when you are feeling blue, and remembering good times from the past is more pleasant than thinking about what is going on today.

Studies have shown that a walk down memory lane can be good for your health and give your spirits a lift. According to an article in *Psychology Today*, a study done at Loyola University reported that "thinking good memories for just twenty minutes a day can make people more cheerful than they were the week before."[1]

The article continues, "Most people spontaneously reminisce when they're alone or feeling down—or both—which suggests that we reach for pleasant memories as an antidote to feeling blue. . . . Researchers at the University of Southampton in the UK have also found nostalgia to be a potent mood booster. Since memories often star important people in our lives, they may give us a comforting sense of belonging. . . . People who are disposed to experience nostalgia also tend to see their past as positive, adding support to the idea of a nostalgia-prone personality. Previous research has shown that naturally nostalgic people have high self-esteem and are less prone to depression. They cope with problems more effectively and are more likely than not to receive social support after experiencing stress. Not surprisingly, these well-rooted folks also see their families more often."[2]

There are many ways to record fond memories so that they can be remembered in years to come, not only by you as you get older but by your children and their children after you are gone. In addition to scrapbooking and journaling (covered in other chapters in this book), here are a few other suggestions for how to put some sunshine into a rainy afternoon.

Create a library of family photo albums. Organize all those photos you've saved into albums by year or event. Schedule a family time to sit and go through the albums—reminiscing about that fun family vacation, your child's growing up years, special holiday celebrations, and other special memories. Or make a photo montage and frame it for that special place in your home. These are keepsakes that will last for generations to come and will help keep memories alive.

Make a memory quilt. Photos, scraps of material that have special meaning, and memorabilia from special events are all things that can be put into making a quilt. Have different extended family members each create a square, and then patch them together for a beautiful family history.

Make new traditions for the holidays. Try something different each year. Yes, it's important to keep old traditions, but trying new things just might spark a special memory in the future. "Remember that Christmas when . . ." Sue said that when her children were just babies, she started a tradition of buying them each a special Christmas ornament each year with the plan of them each having a box of special ornaments for their tree when they started their own family. "My kids loved these ornaments. As they grew older, I found ornaments that related to what they did that year—soccer, music lessons, baseball, and so on. When they were teens, one of our favorite traditions was to go ornament shopping, when they picked out an ornament that had special meaning to them."

Name a star for your loved one. Here's a unique gift idea that is sure to evoke fond memories for years to come. Several organizations online will name a star and then provide such information as the star name and date and a sky chart showing the constellation it is found in with the specific location marked. If you do this, it's likely that you'll see your loved one searching the heavens for "their star" when they're out at night.

Have an annual retreat with friends. Gatherings are wonderful places to share memories and to record them for posterity. Linda tells of six special friends who get together every year at a cabin in the mountains just to relax and have fun. The "girls' weekend" has been occurring for eight years, and with their busy schedules, this is often the only time all of them get together during the year. Over the years there have been births and deaths, marriages and divorces, happy events and sad events to share, all recorded chronologically in their memories.

Videotape a message. If you want to be remembered long after you're gone, videotape a message to your family and friends. Now is your time to shine as the "star" as you share your life, hopes, and dreams with those you love. It's also a great time to share your faith and what God has meant to you in your life's journey by telling stories of those special times when he has met you in your sorrows and your joys.

Making memories doesn't have to be expensive or time consuming. Tucking an "I love you" note in someone's lunch just might make their day and be a memory they call on when times are rough. When you do something special with a friend or loved one, collect memorabilia such as ticket stubs, menus, receipts, and so on, and put them in a scrapbook or picture frame. The specialness of the event will live on forever.

The ideas for making a memory are limited only by your imagination and creativity. Do something special for yourself or someone else—go make a memory.

IF YOU WANT TO FEEL GREAT TODAY . . .

Keep your terrific memories fresh and crisp. Make them into a tangible memory experience you can enjoy again and again. Don't let life just happen. Be proactive about creating special memories with those you love. Making new memories adds joy to life and overcomes sadness about the bygone days. Preserve your memories with scrapbooks, journaling, or even a picture library.

Remember: You Can't Stay Mad at Someone Who Makes You Laugh

He deserves Paradise who makes his companions laugh.
— Anonymous

SOME TIME AGO, DAVE WAS ASKED TO ADDRESS a group of colleagues who market a whole-food concentrate. With his wacky sense of humor, he thought he would give them a farfetched explanation for why he had joined their effort, so he said something like this: "I was looking for a way to augment my income. I considered establishing a string of 'Insty-Fix Hernia Transplant Centers,' but I found this company instead."

Then he embellished a humorous anecdote he had read and told them about his childhood, when his family was quite poor. "My dad was a minister in a small town in Vermont," he said, "so every week when other people would wash their clothes for church in their washing machines, we would join the other poor folk and wash our clothes in the river. Most of the rest used soap and rocks they brought along to beat the dirt out, but we were so poor we didn't have any rocks, so we had to beat our clothes with our heads."[1]

The first part didn't inspire anybody. But they laughed at the poor-boy story and also at his statement that his wife had recently said that he was getting fat, and when he asked how fat, she had said "seven months," so he thought perhaps he should make an appointment with an ob-gyn. As a result of that little bit of frivolity, someone referred to him later as "our stand-up comic," and just about any time during the next few days that he encountered people who had been at that session, they would smile at him, and he at them. In fact, this so inspired him that when he received the microphone again toward the end of the conference and was asked if he had anything to say about the achievement that was being celebrated, he said that first of all, he wanted to thank his mother for having him.

It's fun to make people laugh, and it's healthy, too—perhaps more for them than for you, but it will brighten your day. When you make someone laugh, you're helping them to be healthier. A wide range of studies have shown the following positive effects when someone laughs:

- **Increased pain tolerance**—after all, it's hard to remember that you've got a broken toe when you're laughing like a madman, don't you think?
- **Reduced stress**—seems like this should go without saying, although sometimes it's embarrassing when you start to laugh at the worst possible moment as a defense mechanism.
- **Increased immunity**—since stress reduction, however it happens, improves one's immunity.
- **Increased circulation**—as evidenced by how people gasp for breath when they're having a good belly laugh.

- **Burning of calories**—maybe a lot, depending on how long and hard you laugh, since a ten-minute belly laugh burns the equivalent of one bite of a Snickers candy bar.

As Dave was drafting this chapter, his brother e-mailed him a wacko semi-humorous story that he won't repeat, but it was difficult to hold back at least a little wry smile. And then he sent back a funnier story (in his opinion) than he had received. Without a doubt, the Internet and e-mail have made it possible to make somebody laugh, whether they're two thousand miles away or halfway around the world, simply by finding something funny and passing it along. And with that click of the mouse, you've brightened somebody's day (and your own).

Of course, certain people have a gift for making others laugh. One of Dave's friends, John, can make Dave laugh so hard and for so long (in person) that he has to beg John to stop. But Dave gets John back whenever he can by sending him the best stuff that comes his way, including the following purportedly true examples of federal employee evaluations:

- His men would follow him anywhere, but only out of morbid curiosity.
- This young lady has delusions of adequacy.
- He sets low personal standards and then consistently fails to achieve them.
- This employee is depriving a village somewhere of an idiot.
- He's been working with glue too much.
- He has a knack for making strangers immediately.

And Dave's all-time favorite from this list (which is just one of many you can find on the Internet): He would argue with a signpost.

If these made you laugh, great—because, like it says in the book of Proverbs, "A merry heart doeth good like a medicine" (17:22, KJV).

Here are just a few ideas of how to use humor to elicit a guffaw or two from somebody else:

- Keep a clown nose in your pocket, and if things get tense at home or work, stick it on. After all, as Jay Leno said, "You can't stay mad at somebody who makes you laugh."
- Wear a humorous T-shirt and laugh along with those who read it.
- Place a classified ad like the following allegedly actual ads, and then have a good laugh if anyone calls: "Frozen bath tissue, 4 rolls: 89 cents"; "Used frost-free microwave"; "Free can of baked beans with purchase of two-bath home."
- And Dave's all-time favorite, that he's not yet had the guts to try—sit in your bathrobe in a lawn chair on your front lawn and point your hair dryer at your neighbors as they go by in their cars on their way to work.

IF YOU WANT TO FEEL GREAT TODAY . . .

Incite some chortling! Go out of your way to make people smile. It won't cost anything and will make you both happier. Encourage your own wacky sense of humor and pass on those stories and jokes. Remember that laughter not only boosts your health but even burns calories.

24

Invest Yourself

A lot of people have gone further than they thought they could because someone else thought they could.

– Anonymous

PERHAPS YOU CAN REMEMBER PEOPLE IN YOUR own life who believed in you enough to encourage you and to share the wisdom of their own expertise and experience. The original "Mentor" was a character in Homer's poem *The Odyssey*. When Odysseus, King of Ithaca, went on his various travels and to fight in the Trojan War, he entrusted the care of his kingdom and his son, Telemachus, to his wise and trusted counselor, Mentor.[1]

Traditionally, mentoring has been described as "the activities conducted by a person (the mentor) for another person (the mentee or protégé) in order to help that other person to do a job more effectively and/or progress in their career. The mentor was probably someone who had 'been there, done that' before. A mentor might use a variety of approaches, e.g., coaching, training, discussion, counseling."[2]

The terms coaching and mentoring are often used interchangeably, but coaches do not need any special experience within the area in which they are offering support, whereas mentors are experts within a particular field. Coaching concentrates on specific goals with clear outcomes. Mentoring is usually part of a longer term developmental path, with outcomes less defined than those of coaching. Coaching is usually "time bound" with a specific duration relating to the defined goals, whereas mentoring relationships can go on for a long time and may see progress through many stages and in many arenas of life, including character development.[3]

Mentoring is often less formal than coaching, such as when an adult comes alongside a troubled teen and offers guidance, help, and the chance to interact with a positive role model. Many cities have Big Brothers Big Sisters programs that provide these services. Some churches, particularly those in inner city areas, also provide these types of programs.

Rex has become a mentor to troubled teens in his own town. A year after the suicide of his son, Rex began volunteering at a local continuation high school, working with at-risk kids from troubled backgrounds who had themselves been in trouble, often as a result of diagnosed or undiagnosed mental disorders and other issues that had kept them from performing well in a normal school setting. Rex has spent many hours with these students, talking to them, taking them fishing at the local lake, and most important of all, listening to them and encouraging them as they've told their stories. He does what he does best: "talking a little and listening a lot."

For his investment of time, he was honored as "high school volunteer of the year" by the local school district. Even more important to him than that honor, however, is knowing that he is making a difference in the lives of young people. He knows he's helping others, and this has become one of the ways he feels like he is making a difference as a result of his son's death.

....

Being mentored is an invaluable opportunity to grow and learn from someone who has wisdom and expertise to offer. Also, those who are being mentored often have no other positive role model, and many report that they don't know the direction their lives would have taken if their mentor had not come alongside them and poured heart and soul into their lives.

Perhaps you're intrigued by this idea but wonder if you have what it takes. Obviously, the most important characteristic of a mentor is the desire to help and to be involved in the lives of others. Often mentors are those who have had a positive experience with a mentor in their own life and are willing to "pay it forward." In other words, they want to give back to others what they have received. A mentor is someone, like Rex, who has the time and energy, both physical and emotional, to devote to the mentoring relationship. Mentors don't necessarily have to have all the answers as long as they are willing and able to learn, sometimes from their own protégés, so it's a process that benefits both parties.

Although most people begin a mentoring relationship with the idea of giving to someone else and don't usually consider what they themselves might gain, in a professional setting there is the opportunity to enhance your own professional growth by strengthening your coaching and leadership skills. Mentoring in this setting can also improve your performance by motivating you to set a good example and to work harder. It can provide a fresh perspective on your performance and help you keep your own skills and thinking sharp.[4]

One mentor said, "Becoming a mentor is satisfying because the person you are helping is letting you know that you are someone they admire and hold in high regard. Mentoring is really an endorsement for you because it says that someone looks up to you and views you as someone they can learn from."[5]

Perhaps the greatest and best-known mentor was Jesus of

Nazareth. During the three years of his ministry, he handpicked his followers and then mentored, trained, and taught them, preparing them to carry on his work. Not only did those men benefit from his teaching, but they then mentored and taught others, who then mentored and taught others, and so on, which is one reason the Christian faith is still vibrant more than two thousand years after Jesus's death.

In the New Testament, the apostle Paul described this process of multiplication to his own protégé, a younger man named Timothy: "And the things you have heard me say in the presence of many witnesses entrust to reliable men who will also be qualified to teach others" (2 Timothy 2:2, NIV).

IF YOU WANT TO FEEL GREAT TODAY . . .

Become a mentor. Invest yourself in others. Examine your areas of expertise to discover knowledge or skills you would like to pass on. Be alert to those around you who could forge ahead, with the help of some mentoring. Also, be aware of people around you who have skill or knowledge you would like to acquire, and ask them to mentor you.

········· **25** ·········

Make the "E" Word Your Servant, Not Your Master

You cannot make yourself feel something you do not feel, but you can make yourself do right in spite of your feelings.
– Pearl S. Buck

MOST PEOPLE WOULD LOVE TO FEEL HAPPY, loved, and on top of the world all the time, but it just isn't possible. Life happens, and no matter how good we feel one minute, circumstances can send us spiraling the next. In fact, it's quite common to feel one emotion and later, perhaps the same day, feel much different. For example, it's not uncommon to experience happiness at an enjoyable event and not long after that to have a letdown and feel sad or exhausted.

A mood is a state of mind. If we are happy, in love, or excited, our mood is usually elevated and light. If we are angry, sad, or fearful, our mood may be dark and depressed. Even if our mood is negative for a while, it can become more positive again if we have learned to handle our emotions.

Many factors can determine how much control we have over

our emotions, but perhaps the most significant is experience. For example, we've all seen a two-year-old carrying on in a grocery store because he or she absolutely must have that item now, or (apparently, based on the noise) life will lose its meaning. Depending on the result, the child's perspective is reinforced, or the child learns that life can still be happy without that lollypop.

If we were raised in a positive, loving, nurturing atmosphere, we usually carry these perspectives into adulthood and are better able to apply a positive outlook to our circumstances. On the other hand, if our home life was abusive, negative, or critical, we have to work harder to have a positive outlook on life and what it brings to us day by day.

Researchers have done countless studies on the role that emotions play in healing, finding that those with a positive outlook heal faster and better. Our physical health can also affect how we feel emotionally. For example, if we have chronic pain, it is more difficult to maintain a positive outlook. It's also important to examine our relationships. Do we keep company with negative, critical, "glass half empty" people? Or do we hang out with people who are positive, who are going places, and who look at life from the "glass half full" perspective?

Our feelings and emotions are a response to our thoughts and beliefs. What we think plays out in how we feel, which then affects our behavior. In order to change our behavior, we need to change our thinking. By the time we reach adulthood, we are pretty well programmed to think the way we do. Women have a tendency to stuff their true feelings, and men have a tendency to express their feelings in angry outbursts or other negative behavior instead of recognizing and speaking their true feelings.

Sometimes, for one reason or another, a person's "feeling vocabulary" is limited. We know of one person who was working with a counselor to try to resolve some negative emotions about an extremely trying event that had happened. Each week when the client came in, the counselor would ask, "How are you feeling?" and the person would respond, "I don't know." The counselor knew that the issue was finding the right word, so each week he would review a list of feeling words, and when he hit the right one, the person agreed that was accurate. Then they could discuss what was happening. Such a list of feeling words is not as limitless as you might think, though there isn't room to list them all here. There are pleasant feelings, with major headings like open, happy, alive, good, love, interested, positive, or strong. There are unpleasant feeling words like angry, depressed, confused, helpless, indifferent, afraid, hurt, or sad. Each of these, whether positive or negative, has a subset of words with more refined but related meanings.

The best way to deal with feelings is to recognize and name them and then learn to speak of them in ways that others can understand and not feel threatened by. It's analogous to a doctor coming up with a diagnosis (i.e., naming a condition) so that he or she and the team trying to help you can then deal with the cause.

With feelings, this can be done in several ways. Trace your negative feelings back to their source. Ask yourself, "What thoughts are causing these feelings?" It may be helpful to get off by yourself to process this. It may also be helpful to journal, writing out your thoughts. If you're angry that your spouse or children did not help with the dinner dishes, instead of lashing out at them and blaming them for their insensitivity, you might ask yourself, "What is really going on here? Why am I angry? Did I have a difficult day at work? Is someone in my family ill and I'm concerned? Did a friend treat me badly?"

If, through this self-examination, you decide that you are tired, feel unappreciated, and need more help from your family, sit down with them and express how you feel. Make "I" statements ("I've got a lot going on right now because of _____, and I really need more help from each of you"). Don't place blame on others because of how you feel. Express your true feelings and ask for help.

Some people tend to relive their past failures and hurts, which can send them spiraling into depression. Practice "thought stopping." When those automatic thoughts enter your mind, say, "Stop. If I go down that path, I know where it will lead me." Remember, you can't change the past, but you can learn from it and do better in the future. A good rule of thumb: Don't believe everything you think.

Dan was a recovering alcoholic who came from an abusive background. He was a product of his past and desperately wanted to end the cycle and move forward. However, he was a victim of his thinking, which made it difficult for him to deal positively with his emotions and behavior. Then, he said, "I started journaling my thoughts, tracing them to their origins, and practiced stopping them from going further. I taught myself to focus on the positive things going on in my life." Today Dan has a good job and a family who loves him. He still struggles with his thinking process, but it no longer controls him. He has control over it.

Naming your feelings is the first step to changing them.

IF YOU WANT TO FEEL GREAT TODAY . . .

Realize that you are not a slave to the "E" word. Let your emotions inform you, then claim how you feel. Use that energy to engage them appropriately. You don't have to allow a negative feeling to become a mood. A mood is a state of mind, but feelings are changeable and reflect thoughts and beliefs. To maintain positive and encouraging thoughts, gravitate toward positive people and away from those who drag you down.

.... **26** ....

Put on Your Own Mask First

You were made for enjoyment and the world was filled with things which you will enjoy.
— John Ruskin

WHEN WAS THE LAST TIME YOU TOOK THE time to do something nice for yourself, not because, in the words of the ad, "you're worth it," but because you need it? Of course you are too busy—most of the time. You have a job, family, friends, home, and other responsibilities that leave you too little time for "frivolous" things.

If this describes you, we have a question: Is it responsible to take care of yourself—your needs, wants, and desires—so that you will be in a better place to meet similar needs, wants, and desires in others?

Few have learned the art of taking care of themselves so that they can better take care of others. If you've flown, you are well aware of the rule to put your own oxygen mask on first and then take care of others. The same principle applies to the rest of your life: when you are healthier and happier because you are taking care of yourself, you are better equipped to take care of others' needs as well.

Research has shown that there are significant health benefits to eating right, getting enough sleep, exercising, keeping your mind focused on healthy and positive things, nurturing your spirit with prayer and quiet time, staying connected with family and friends, and taking time out to just have fun. Taking time to pamper yourself can add to these benefits, as many are discovering.

"Visits to health spas in the United States have increased by almost 60 percent since 1997, according to a recent survey by the International Spa Association. The top three reasons for going? Pampering massage, stress reduction and pain relief. While massaging your own back may prove next to impossible, you can easily and affordably reap the benefits of stress reduction and pain relief in your home hot tub, steam unit or sauna. . . . If insomnia is stressing you out, you've got one more reason to immerse yourself in steam. A 1999 study conducted by Harvard physician Cynthia Dorsey, PhD, director of the Sleep Research Program at McLean Hospital in Belmont, Massachusetts, found that 30-minute steam baths taken 1.5 to two hours before bedtime improved sleep efficiency in female insomniacs by approximately 10 percent."[1]

Although saunas and steam bathing are not for everyone and should be avoided by those with heart conditions and diabetes and by women who are pregnant, a warm bath can do wonders for stress. Get out your favorite bath oils, bubbles, and scented soap and take a long soak in the tub. Placing some scented candles around the room along with playing soft music helps add to the ambience and helps you soak away the stress and cares of the world. Doing this before you go to bed might help you get a better night's sleep.

Pampering isn't just for women. In addition to trying spas and saunas, men are turning up in record numbers at nail salons for manicures and pedicures and are seeking massages as frequently as women. Many cosmetics companies now have skin-care lines for men. Men are seeing the added benefits of taking care of themselves.

Here are some great ideas for pampering yourself:

- Get a manicure or pedicure. These are relatively inexpensive and don't have to be done every week. "I have very weak nails, which crack and split when left to themselves. My hands are in front of people all the time," said Sue. "One of the few extras my budget allows is getting my nails done. I feel good knowing my nails look good."
- Do a facial at home. Cleanse your skin well with a good cleaning product. Next, rub in a gentle exfoliating scrub, rinsing your face well afterwards. Steam your face with a warm wash cloth. Apply a mask appropriate for your skin's needs. Leave the mask on for fifteen to twenty minutes, then rinse your face well. Apply a good moisturizer. You'll feel like a new person.
- Take care of your feet. Soak them to soften the skin, then use a pumice stone to slough off dead skin. Finish with a good foot cream.
- Get a massage. This can be done by a professional or with one of the many home massage tools that can be purchased relatively inexpensively. This is a good stress reliever and will help with those sore, aching muscles.
- Deep condition your hair. This can be done while taking that warm, relaxing bath.
- Get a haircut, a new color, or even a new style. Have you been wearing your hair in the same old way for years? Maybe a new style will give you that needed pick-me-up. Debbie said, "I think the reason that getting my hair done makes me feel good is because when I go there is about two months' worth of growth. When I get it colored, it hides all the gray that makes me feel

old, and this helps me to maybe hide the inevitable. I really don't wear my hair the same way for long. I feel like it is a canvas, a blank slate. When I walk out of the shop it is like a fresh start. It just makes me feel good."

- Relax. Instead of starting dinner when you get home from a busy day, lie down on the couch for a few minutes for some quiet time. Read a book or listen to a relaxing CD if you want. This is a good time to teach your children, if they are in the home, the importance of relaxation. Purpose to use one day a week to relax and rest from all your labors, and use the time to renew your relationship with God and your loved ones.
- Take time to reflect on all the positive things in your life. Write in your journal. Keep a list of things you are thankful for.

IF YOU WANT TO FEEL GREAT TODAY . . .

Airline attendants tell us that in case of a drop in cabin pressure, we should put on our own mask before trying to assist others. That's good advice, and it applies to life. You can't help others if you're incapacitated. If your own batteries are low, how can you recharge others? So go ahead and pamper yourself a bit. This will restore your energy, improve your mood, and enhance your overall health. Try a manicure, pedicure, facial, massage, or relax with a good book. Don't listen to those voices in your own mind saying these things are vain, frivolous, or wasteful. If they restore your vitality, you'll be able to uplift others, and that's a good thing!

27

Enjoy the Ornithological Sideshow

I hope you love birds, too. It is economical. It saves going to heaven.
                                                              – Emily Dickinson

SOMETIMES CHANGING YOUR FOCUS WILL miraculously change your mood. Right outside your window is an amazing community of feathered friends just waiting to entertain you. Winter, spring, summer, or fall you can become a part of their habitat and busy schedule. Most of us have enjoyed seeing the careful building of a nest followed by the excitement of the eggs hatching and then relished a front-row seat as the little ones began their flying lessons. But have you ever actually become a part of the process? Nature lovers across the country go one step beyond bird watching and enmesh themselves in the daily activities of these amazing creatures.

Bird watching is an ideal solitary or shared activity. It is the fastest-growing outdoor activity in America, with 51.3 million Americans now taking part. Your senses open up, and your mind settles down. You concentrate not only on the beauty and power of the birds around you but also on their beautiful songs. Observing birds is reported to have a soothing effect upon the body, mind, and spirit.

Bill, a friend of ours, is fascinated by hummingbirds. The smallest of the bird family, hummingbirds dart about on their wings at warp speed. In studying their life cycle and habitat, Bill was motivated to build a bit of a hummingbird paradise in the yard of their lake cottage. He planted hummingbird-preferred flowers (red is their favorite color) and got special feeders designed for their tiny size. He learned about their favorite sweet nectar drink, which he then faithfully concocted and supplied to the flocks. The result was hours of enjoyment for him and his family and the many friends and neighbors who love to visit his hummingbird haven.

Another family saved pieces of colored yarn and cloth and put them out for possible nest-building materials. It was a thrill to see Mrs. Robin choose a bit of cloth from a child's favorite outgrown shirt to decorate her nest. By the end of nest-building time, the family could spot bright colors in the trees about their yard, gathered from their contributions! Other families have a Thanksgiving tradition of decorating a small evergreen in their yard with treats for the birds. Making pinecone peanut butter ornaments as an early Christmas present for the birds is a great way to entertain younger children.

In the winter you can bring the bird antics and parade of colors right to your window. Finches, for instance, are lively and come arrayed in gorgeous colors. Nuthatches are the clowns in the bird world, as they perform amazing acrobatic feats for our viewing pleasure. A bird bath is a great addition to any yard and will allow lots of laughs as you observe the bathing routines of the different species. Choosing the species of bird you want to attract will dictate which seeds you supply to your hungry visitors.

It is thrilling to watch throngs of birds flock to the shelter of a huge evergreen tree just before a big snowfall. They continue their lively banter and dance as they flit about without a care as the storm rages. Or how about the fun of observing the preparations for the flight south in the fall? When our (Jim and Bobbie's) children were young we would all watch with anticipation the "bird good-bye party." The loud chatter goes on for days as more and more flocks gather in the trees of their staging area. Practicing short flights comes next, and you can envision different leaders trying out for the lead position. They eat gourmet meals and strengthen and practice different flight techniques, all amid the constant chatter. Then the day comes when the invisible signal is given, and, in one enormous winged cloud, they rise simultaneously to begin their arduous journey to a warmer climate. An eerie silence then settles over the treetops, and we always feel a bit of longing as our feathered friends fly away toward sunnier lands.

For many, just watching birds in their backyard is not enough; they long to actually be in the center of a winged world. Some hikers climb to places where they can have a bird's-eye view. One short hike in Washington State will take you to such a place, and as you near the end of the trail you find yourself at the top of a ridge where a gorge runs down into the river below. It is a bird playground, and you will be spellbound as you observe the beauty of the soaring marbled murrelets or hermit warblers. You may even catch a glimpse of a majestic bald eagle as it glides about its daily activities. Such an experience is guaranteed to change your day as you are rejuvenated by such spectacular sights.

No matter where you live, scores of birds are just waiting to be discovered. Birding even satisfies our primal hunting instincts as the different species are tracked. Many states organize festivals to celebrate their feathered inhabitants. Cape May, New

Jersey, for instance, hosts a spring weekend to welcome the birds back home in the month of May. You will be sure to see a variety of shorebirds unique to the saltwater marsh such as the osprey, heron, oystercatcher, gull, and tern. Watch for the comical march of the sandpipers as they parade along the water's edge gathering breakfast and dodging waves.

Reading about birds is a great pastime in itself, since studying the habits of some birds can yield surprising results. Recently German researchers observed that birds use the same technique as humans to catch up on lost sleep—the power nap! Birds are the only animals other than mammals who demonstrate both slow-wave sleep and rapid eye movement, which is characteristic of dreaming. Don't you wonder what they dream about?

Take delight in the drama all around you the next time you are feeling bored or lonely. God made an ornithological sideshow for all of us to enjoy. It is free, can be done any day of the year from any location, and may even introduce you to some new human companions through the birding groups in your community. Get your binoculars, and we will see you out there.

IF YOU WANT TO FEEL GREAT TODAY . . .

Change your focus from your four walls inside to the birds' three ring circus outside. Bird watching is an ideal solitary or shared activity. Try watching the birds to open up your senses and settle your mind. Challenge your brain with learning facts about the different species and identifying them. Let your spirit soar with them in delight.

Seek Buried Treasure

Squire Trelawney, Dr. Livesey, and the rest of these gentlemen having asked me to write down the whole particulars about Treasure Island, from the beginning to the end, keeping nothing back but the bearings of the island, and that only because there is still treasure not yet lifted. . . .

— Opening lines of Treasure Island
by Robert Louis Stevenson

I MAGINE THIS: ON YOUR TWELFTH BIRTHDAY YOU get a letter from your grandfather who passed away several years ago, addressed to you and marked "confidential." In the envelope is a piece of paper and a piece of deerskin, on which is sketched a map from your back porch to clue number one. Your grandpa wrote: "When you were born, I purchased a U.S. savings bond in your name, which, if you allow it to mature, will pay for your first year of college. I buried it in a safe place. Now all you have to do is find it!"

Clue number one leads you off your back porch, thirty paces directly west, then north one hundred paces. Clue number two is hidden among the roots of a maple tree within thirty feet of your position. But you look around and don't see any maple tree, though there are a few stumps in a newly logged clearing. What now? How far do you pursue this, and whose help do you enlist? You're on a hunt, and the prize is substantial. This is better than the treasure of the Sierra Madre, Captain Kidd's buried treasure, or even becoming a raider of the lost ark. This is real. Your grandpa, who was a novelist of some repute, knew about adventure and intrigue and how to give you a day you would never forget.

If you're having a blah day, here's a surefire way to change that, and fast: create a treasure hunt for your kids, your grandkids, or your neighbor's kids. It doesn't matter so much who you do it for, just that you do it, and then savor the increasing excitement as the participants get closer to the treasure—clue by clue.

Everyone loves a treasure hunt, with its mystery and intrigue, sometimes romance and conflict between good and evil, and clues that must be deciphered in the hope of finding that treasure, whatever it may be. One of the parables of Jesus describes the kingdom of heaven as being like a treasure that a man found hidden in a field (see Matt. 13:44). The man went and spent all he had in order to buy that field. Isn't it possible that our enjoyment of the hunt for treasure is built into us by our Creator, with the goal of setting us all on the greatest treasure hunt of all—the search for truth?

It's not hard to create a treasure hunt, regardless of where you live. If you do a Google search with the phrase "how to create a treasure hunt," you'll find over 200,000 entries, enough ideas for a lifetime of making life fun for a veritable gaggle of little friends—and also for yourself.

One of our colleagues created treasure hunts for his children as they were growing up in Colorado. The hunt might start with some kind of discovery the kids had already made in the nearby woods. For example, one day when our friend's son, Travis, was about ten, the boy found a very old axe in the woods and brought it home to show his father. "I was building a fort next to the ledge when I found this," Travis explained. "You said that Jesse James used to hang out around here. Do you think this might have been his axe, Papa? Do you?"

The family was actually living on part of an old Colorado ranch located in an area that had been one of Jesse James's old haunts. "At that moment, an idea crystallized in my mind," our friend wrote, "to design a treasure hunt and keep this excitement of discovery and imagination alive as long as possible while at the same time teaching Travis and our daughter Heather a little history, orienteering, biology, logic, reading, and research. I shook my head slowly, pondering the possibilities. 'I don't know, Travis,' I replied. 'But it sure looks like it's old enough to have been here when he was alive.'"

Following that assertion, the father invested his next three days in secretly placing leather map fragments, antique bottles, artifacts, and a sealed wooden box containing pre-1900 coins wrapped in an old canvas bag in various places near the spot where the axe had been found. He chipped clues into cliff faces and then glued moss back on to give the clues the appearance of age. When he was done, even a bear track at the spring hole and a bottle carefully placed under the roots of a tree were among the clues and along the trail to the treasure.

As you can imagine, the kids had a wonderful time unraveling the mystery, learning a lot about teamwork as they went. But the father also experienced an intense sense of anticipation in the process of creating the hunt and then, as he followed at a distance, observing his children and two of their friends finding the clues and, ultimately, the treasure. He even let them believe for several days that they had found the treasure of Jesse James.

"They had a wonder-filled day," he wrote, "and mine was just plain wonder-full."

Of course, not everyone has access to history, legends, or artifacts like these, but you can discover some local lore with a little mystery (or create your own through storytelling), and then develop a hunt that will test the kids but not frustrate them too much.

"Success depends on the combination of just enough suspense and difficulty to keep them wondering," our friend concluded, "plus an increasing set of rewards that will keep them motivated to reach the final goal—the treasure."[1]

If or when you do this, remember that the real treasure is the making of a memory, the shared joy, the fun, the laughter—relational values that cannot be bought at any price. And keep in mind that this particular way to make your day great can be spread over several days or even a week as you work out the "hunt" piece by piece, resulting in a whole bunch of "great" days, all from one source.

IF YOU WANT TO FEEL GREAT TODAY . . .

Infuse your day with creativity and excitement by creating a treasure hunt for someone you care about. Designing a treasure map or hunt is mental exercise, engaging many areas of your brain. Planning a treasure hunt for a child helps keep you young. Then, through the years, the memory of the experience will remain, long after the treasure has been found . . . or perhaps the real treasure is in the memory itself.

Play for Your Own Enjoyment and Amazement

I play a musical instrument a little, but only for my own amazement. — Fred Allen, American comedian

PERHAPS BACK IN YOUR SCHOOL DAYS YOU played an instrument in the band or orchestra. But then you put that instrument away and you haven't touched it since. Or perhaps you took piano lessons at the insistence of your parents, who told you, "Someday you'll be glad you did this." Just thinking about playing scales brings back memories of hours of practice while your friends were outside playing. Many have reported that they are glad they took those lessons because they play now as adults, while others haven't touched a piano since they finally convinced their parents they were not Bach or Beethoven, never would be, and didn't want to be.

Maybe you never had the opportunity to take music lessons or play in a band and would love to learn to play an instrument for your own enjoyment. Many adults are signing up for piano lessons because they have found that they really want to play, whereas many kids don't. Because of the Internet, adults have become aware that piano lessons don't have to happen in a music studio or store. They can learn at their own pace through lessons available on the Internet. Traditional methods of learning by reading music and practicing scales are not the only way to learn to play. Learning chords and chording techniques, available on the Internet, is a viable option. Adults are discovering that piano playing is something relaxing they can do after work. Some become good enough to play at social events, at parties, in their churches, and so on. Lessons taken in this manner are also less expensive than traditional lessons.[1]

However, learning to play an instrument as an adult has its own set of challenges. Bob Karlovits, a music writer for the *Pittsburgh Tribune-Review*, wrote, "Adults often begin the study of music despite challenges that seem daunting. The practice that can be accomplished easily by a youngster is more difficult for a person dealing with a mortgage, career, and a family. Christine Morris, director of the Westmoreland Suzuki School of Music, says adults 'often need more encouragement' than children do because they expect to be able to conquer musical frontiers more quickly." On the plus side, adults are more goal-oriented than kids and know what they want and who they'd like to emulate with their music-playing ability.[2]

Making music is good for your health. "Studies show that active music making (not passive music listening) correlates with: increased spatial-temporal reasoning and better math scores, better reading ability, lower incidence of drug use and antisocial behavior, and increased wellness."[3] *Music of the Heart* is a film about Roberta Guaspari, a violin teacher who took her music to the inner-city schools of New York. Her goal was to brighten the lives of disadvantaged students. Since the program began in 1991, hundreds of students have learned to play the violin and other instruments. The philosophy of Guaspari's Opus 118

Harlem School of Music is that "Learning a musical instrument is a unique way of exposing children to beauty" and that "Music education creates and expands horizons for children who would otherwise lack the opportunity to experience the benefits that are derived from such an education."[4]

The American Music Conference states that playing an instrument has many benefits for all ages, even the elderly. "Senior citizens who are actively involved in music making enjoy significant health benefits. For example, studies show that music activates the cerebellum and therefore may aid stroke victims [in regaining] language capabilities. . . . Studies show improvements in the brain chemistry of people suffering from Alzheimer's . . . [and] that older Americans who are actively involved in music show improvements in anxiety, loneliness, and depression—three factors that are critical in coping with stress, stimulating the immune system, and improving health. A breakthrough study demonstrated that group keyboard lessons given to older Americans had a significant effect on increasing levels of human growth hormone (hGh), which is implicated in such aging phenomena as osteoporosis, energy levels, wrinkling, sexual function, muscle mass, and aches and pains."[5]

"I hated piano lessons when I was a kid," said Ivy. "However, when I decided to study music in college, I was glad I had them. Those lessons prepared me to play at my church, to teach piano lessons, and to learn other instruments as an adult. It has been much easier to pick up the guitar, for example, because I have a background in music. I recently purchased a dulcimer and am taking lessons. There is a dulcimer group in my community that gets together once a month. We are all at different levels, but it is fun to play with those who have been playing for years. They are very patient with those of us who are learning. Playing an instrument helps with the normal stresses of life. It helps me relax, as well as giving me self-confidence when I've had a hard day at work. I believe that children need something they are good at so that when life falls apart around them, they have something to fall back on. Playing an instrument fits this need."

How do you decide which instrument to try? The American Music Conference says, "Pretty simple: you try what interests you. And if that doesn't feel right, you try something else."[6] If you have an instrument, that might make your choice easier. Cost is a factor—purchasing a piano might not be in your budget. However, you might consider renting or borrowing a keyboard and starting there. "Between friends, family and special music store rentals, it is possible to get the feel of any instrument before you actually purchase one." Often music stores will let you take an instrument for a "test drive." Your local retailer can do more than just sell you an instrument. Most music stores offer a complete learning experience—many offer rentals, trial periods, group and individual lessons, and other services that help you not only get what you really want, but also to get the most out of it.

Many communities have recreational music groups for several different types of instruments, such as Ivy's community has for the dulcimer. Do an Internet search and find out what your community has to offer. Not only is making music good for your health, it is a social outlet as well.

IF YOU WANT TO FEEL GREAT TODAY . . .

Make music. Learn to play a new instrument or relearn one you used to play. You are never too old to learn how to play an instrument. Soon you, too, can be making beautiful music! Music played or sung by you is therapy for your own heart and soul.

.... **30** ....

Try the Nonfattening, Noninvasive, Performance-Enhancing, Mood-Lifter

Nappers are never caught napping because there is no crime to catch. Nappers are merely seen napping.
— *William A. Anthony*

FEELING CRANKY? HAVING TROUBLE FINISHING that project that must be done today? Chances are you did not sleep well last night, and now you are paying the piper. Some people falsely believe that a nap will rob them of a good night's sleep or, worse yet, make them too exhausted to finish out their day. But the right kind of nap can improve your work performance without interfering with your sleep. Research has discovered that if we follow the rules of napping, we will be more alert, more productive, healthier, and a lot less cranky.

A proper nap should last only fifteen to twenty-five minutes and should be taken when our natural rhythm dips, usually after lunch. One of our "napster" friends reports that eighteen minutes is his own perfect nap length. Some of the bad PR about napping has been formulated from those experiences when the napper "overdoses" and wakes up an hour or two later feeling groggy and out of sorts. This sleep inertia usually only lasts twenty to thirty minutes but is nonexistent if we only nap for thirty minutes max, which is enough to rejuvenate us.

Bill and Camille Anthony, founders of The Napping Company, are great believers in guilt-free naps at work and at home. They promise that naps, in addition to enhancing mood and performance, are no cost, no sweat, nonfattening, noninvasive, and proven to have no dangerous side effects! They are advocates for Workplace Napping Days during which businesses and organizations celebrate the day with company-wide lunches followed by a Nap-a-Thon fundraiser or Napalooza party. Their books *The Art of Napping* and *Workplace Napping* are beloved by many.

Researchers at Harvard and the University of Athens Medical School studied 24,000 Greek adults for six years. Those who took regular thirty-minute midday naps at least three times a week were 37 percent less likely to die of heart disease than other participants. The statistics for working men who napped showed an even greater benefit. Sixty-four percent of this group had a lowered risk of death from heart disease. It is believed that the napping relieved work stress, which can cause problems for the heart.[1] Naps may even help us control our weight gain. Lack of sleep prevents proper balance of the hormones that regulate hunger and satiety, so many are more prone to eating high-calorie snacks when tired.

If naps have all these benefits, why don't more people take advantage of this free, healthy cure for sleep debt? One reason is that napping used to have a very bad reputation. Only the lazy, the sick, or the very old took naps! In addition, life in the U.S. encourages us to be engaged twenty-four hours a day. Shopping malls and restaurants are open far into the night; business goes on in almost every sector 24/7. Twenty-four-hour fitness clubs are all the rage. Hospitals are no longer one of the few entities providing twenty-four-hour services. Even road crews work through the night, digging and paving. It is hard to remember that not too many years ago, most stores closed at 5:00 p.m., and television did not beckon us twenty-four hours a day. Life was simpler, and our bodies had an easier time staying true to our biological clock.

Sandy and Ben had long anticipated their thirtieth-anniversary vacation. Escaping a major snowstorm in Chicago, they looked forward to the week they would be spending in Lahaina, Maui, a small but bustling town. After several fun-packed days of touring, swimming, and shopping, they longed to experience what is described as the "real Hawaii." They set off on the spectacular drive to Hana, famous for its 617 curves and fifty-six one-lane bridges past ocean vistas, tropical forests, and waterfalls. Arriving in peaceful Hana by early evening, they made their way to a small guest house, but to their surprise found everything in the town closed up by 9:00 p.m. The absence of even a television or radio sent them outside for a memorable time of conversation and stargazing as they were lulled by the music of the waves. The next morning they wandered about the tiny village, but by early afternoon they found the shops were all closed for "resting." Feeling like they were on another planet, Sandy and Ben overcame their irritation and embraced the local custom as they stretched out in hammocks under the palm trees to indulge in a long overdue nap!

Naps have long been prescribed for professionals whose alertness can affect the safety of those in their care. Before doctors' work hours became more humane, many interns were expected to grind through eighty- and ninety-hour workweeks. Doctors did their best to overcome grogginess and became experts at ten-minute naps. NASA knows that a nap will improve performance and alertness for sleepy astronauts. Airline pilots are instructed that if they feel fatigued on long flights, they should take a short nap, placing the aircraft in the capable hands of their copilot. This works when the assistant stays alert while the pilot dozes, of course.

A well-planned nap can be part of your arsenal to continue optimal functioning. With a little experimentation, you can discover the best nap strategy for you. If you know you are going to be up later than usual for an event, you may decide to indulge in some planned napping the afternoon before. Many people find this will prevent nodding off in the middle of a concert. Emergency napping is a skill we will all need on occasion. This is the type of napping we can employ when we become sleepy while driving a long distance. Or we can take a siesta at the same time each day. Whatever you decide, always remember that you have a strategy available to get you through. Spending the day groggy and cranky can be avoided. Sleep-deprived citizens of America: plan your guilt-free nap today! And more z's to you!

IF YOU WANT TO FEEL GREAT TODAY . . .

Ask yourself: If there were a medication that would improve job performance and patience, increase alertness, reduce stress and protect against heart disease, while also elevating your mood and helping control your appetite . . . without side-effects . . . would you consider using it? And what if it were also free and available to anyone? Case closed. Take a nap. It's the natural way to rest your mind, rejuvenate your body, and recharge your batteries.

·········· 31 ··········

Acknowledge Your
Need to be Kneaded

I don't fear death because I don't fear anything I don't understand. When I start to think about it, I order a massage and it goes away.
        — Hedy Lamarr, actress

YOU'VE HAD A HARD DAY AT WORK, AND ALL
you want to do is crash on the couch and watch TV.
Your body hurts all over. What do you do? If you're like
many Americans, you might actually opt for the couch, or you
might head out for a full body massage and be glad you did.

According to the American Massage Therapy Association
(AMTA), "in 2007 almost a quarter of adult Americans (24 percent) had a massage at least once in the last 12 months and 34
percent of adult Americans received a massage in the last five
years. Forty-three percent of women and 25 percent of men
have had a massage in the last five years. Baby boomers were
the largest group of people to have received a massage. 90 percent of those polled believed that massage can be beneficial to
your health, and 28 percent ranked medication and massage as

the form of treatment that brought them the greatest relief from pain, followed by chiropractic therapy, physical therapy, and acupuncture."[1]

Massage has come a long way since ancient times when it was usually only an option for the wealthy. Known to have medicinal and beauty benefits, it appears in the writings of many ancient civilizations such as Rome, Greece, Japan, Egypt, China, and India. Massage was introduced in the U.S. by two physicians around the middle of the 1800s. While the practice of massage continued to flourish in other countries, by the 1930s and 1940s American physicians were distracted from the benefits of massage by the explosion of medical advances during these years. Massage, however, remained an important part of the nurse's armament to bring relaxation, pain control, and healing to patients under their care. Many of us have positive memories of the back rubs offered during a hospital stay. During this same period of time, massage gained in popularity among athletes, and finally, in 1996, it was offered as a key treatment during the Summer Olympics. Since that endorsement, massage has been recognized as an important adjunct to our overall health.

If you have never had massage therapy, you may be wondering what all the excitement is about. Why are so many people spending their hard-earned money on massage? Massage has many benefits. It can be used primarily for stress relief and relaxation or as a treatment for conditions involving the ligaments, muscles, tendons, and joints. In the hands of a licensed massage therapist, massage can be used to treat the accumulation of lymph in breast cancer patients. A type of deep-tissue massage can be used to reduce pain and stiffness associated with osteoarthritis. Chinese massage employs two types of muscle stretching and kneading to release various pressure points, which is helpful for patients with fibromyalgia or back pain.

Margaret is eighty-five years old and has been struggling with fibromyalgia for years. Fibromyalgia causes chronic pain in many parts of the body. It can be exacerbated by stress. Margaret said that she has a massage twice a month because it helps loosen tight muscles and helps her relax, thus reducing the pain. She has a massage therapist who comes to her home. "Living on a fixed income, it's sometimes hard to justify the expense. However, I feel so good after my massage that it's even harder to justify not having a massage."

Various research studies have shown massage to reduce anxiety and depression, lower blood pressure, increase circulation, alleviate pain, speed healing after injury, calm fussy babies, and even increase mental performance after a treatment. As always, be wary of any unsubstantiated claims, but realize that massage is fast being incorporated into most pain management programs around the country. Often soothing oils such as lavender, almond, or marjoram are used to further enhance the experience. Are you ready to schedule a massage yet?

The success of your massage therapy will often depend upon the credentials and experience of your therapist. The United States has the highest level of regulation for those who meet the criteria for licensing. Unfortunately, most health insurance providers do not cover the cost of massage, but many businesses have seen the benefits for their employees and offer the service free of charge. Among these forward-looking companies are: JCPenney, Home Depot, FedEx, General Electric, and Yahoo. In 2006, Duke University became one of the forerunners in giving massage, as well as acupuncture and other complementary therapies, the place it deserves in the delivery of integrated medicine. Men have been more reluctant than women to schedule a massage, but, once they do, they are usually repeat customers. Some take awhile to give it a try because, as Dave laughingly reports, when I think of massage, all I can hear is Inspector Clouseau saying, "Do you have for me the 'massage'?"

In all seriousness, definite health benefits come with joining over fifty million of your fellow Americans in having a massage. And, while a massage may seem expensive, perhaps you, like Margaret, can justify the expense as something you are doing to help yourself feel better physically, to reduce stress, and to help you relax. After all, as that famous ad once claimed, "You're worth it." Not only so, but it will definitely improve your day.

IF YOU WANT TO FEEL GREAT TODAY . . .

Get a massage. Arrange to be "kneaded" by someone who knows how to do it well. Many people who believe massage is beneficial to health have never tried it. If you're one of them, before you say that it's too expensive or hard to fit into your schedule, treat yourself, at least once. You'll experience firsthand how the relaxation that massage creates can decrease pain, anxiety, or depression, and . . . leave you feeling great!

32

Be the Bear

*Our deepest fear is not that we are inadequate. Our deepest
fear is that we are powerful beyond measure. It is our light,
not our darkness that most frightens us. . . . Your playing small
does not serve the world. There is nothing enlightened about
shrinking so that other people won't feel insecure around you.
We are all meant to shine, as children do.*

— *Marianne Williamson*

HERE'S THE WAY THIS WORKS: YOUR MIND
whispers, *If I succeed, the expectations of some will rise,
and eventually I will fail and be humiliated. And along
the way I'll make more enemies than friends, because some may
feel put down or shown up and others may see me as a threat.*

The fear of success has received a lot of scientific attention,[1]
since the theory was initially viewed as an explanation for the
slow progress (at that time) of women in business. Although the
theory has come under criticism for various reasons, currently
it is being reconsidered using more modern and highly sophisticated methods of analysis.[2]

I (Dave) recall spending time with a writer who, with his wife,
had created one of the most successful fiction series ever, upon

which one of the most successful series of films ever had been based. Their most recent advance had been in the millions of dollars. Yet when our mutual friend introduced me as a writer, the fellow said, "Ah, a competitor."

A pastor named George and I became friends during our doctoral work. In contrast to the writer just mentioned, George had a unique and totally different approach. "I'm great!" he would proclaim. "I'm so great that it takes a person as great as I am to appreciate how great I am. . . . What? You think I'm great too?! That means that you're great, because you can appreciate how great I am!"[3]

This was George's way of encouraging people with a little humor thrown in. The bottom line message was this: we're children of God and bearers of his image. And since God is love, and God is light, it's okay to let his light and love shine through us so that he will be glorified (see Matt. 5:16; 1 John 1:5; 4:8). George's optimistic and encouraging spirit lifted my spirits during our studies, but not long thereafter my second son almost died, which tapped the grief from the loss of his brother eight years previously. For some time my personal faith light became as dim as it could be without flickering out.

Fast forward seventeen years to 2004. I'm at a party with lots of people, trying to seem sociable enough without actually engaging anyone in meaningful conversation and longing to get back to my little writing and editing "cave," as I call my office in the mountains. I prefer that spot to almost any other except elk camp, which is quieter and even more remote, because I don't have to talk to anybody or see anybody, entertain or try to impress anybody, shower, shave, or even get dressed if I don't feel like it on any given day.

During that party, I notice over the fireplace a very famous limited-edition Thomas Mangelsen photograph entitled "Catch of the Day," in which a grizzly bear that has been waiting at the top of Brooks Falls in Alaska's Katmai National Park is about to catch a salmon that has been struggling very hard to get over the falls and on to the spawning grounds beyond so the salmonic cycle of life can continue.

I ask my host which he most identifies with—the bear or the salmon. He immediately replies, "The bear." This is interesting to me in that whenever I have seen that print before, I have *always* identified with the salmon, with the basic thought, *Yup, that's the way life is. Futility. You overcome multiple obstacles on the journey, but then, just when the goal is in sight, the grim reaper points to YOU.*

That was a few years ago. Today, thanks to knowing and working with this amazing and accomplished young man, I have a poster of a bear about to catch a salmon at Brooks Falls upon which I've written in indelible black magic marker the letters "BTB" for "Be The Bear." And I have a print of the Mangelsen photo hanging in my own living room. My young friend's vitality is infectious, his dreams contagious.

His light has brightened my life so mine can shine God's grace

into the lives of others. And when we shine together, it's a unique and creative synergy that I've never experienced before.

When I think of our friendship, I realize how thankful I am that he (a former Olympic athlete) refused to shrink so I wouldn't feel insecure. He called me out of my cave, step by step, and back into the light. And now I try to replicate this process for others in whom I can see far more potential than they can see in themselves.

You can do the same, but not by hiding and fearing either success or failure. Author John Eldredge, in his book *Wild at Heart*, says we all hunger for the following: a noble battle, an adventure, and beauty to rescue. When you find these things, you shine. You don't play small. You don't shrink. You live bigger, with great resolve, authenticity, clarity, and purpose.

Imagine how you can light up the world. Hold that vision sacred and work toward it with persistence. The world is desperate for more "fully alive" people, people who can make the world a brighter place. You are one of them. So shine on, because, as Marianne Williamson says in the rest of the quote with which we started this chapter, "We were born to make manifest the glory of God that is within us. It's not just in some of us; it's in everyone. And as we let our own light shine, we unconsciously give other people permission to do the same. As we are liberated from our own fear, our presence automatically liberates others."[4]

IF YOU WANT TO FEEL GREAT TODAY . . .

Choose to be the bear instead of the salmon. Let your light and talent shine, because you are one of a kind, unique, and special. Surround yourself with those who inspire you to fear neither success nor failure.

33

Get Off the Gerbil Wheel

The ability to simplify means to eliminate the unnecessary so that the necessary may speak. — Hans Hofmann, artist

ARE YOU IN CONTROL OF YOUR LIFE, OR IS YOUR life controlling you? Perhaps you own too many "toys" that are consuming your time and energy, not to mention your finances. Maybe your job is causing you stress and keeping you from your friends, your family, and the things you enjoy. Sometimes even the people around us can be a drain on our time and energy, especially our emotional energy.

A growing number of people are learning to simplify their lives to reduce stress. "Voluntary simplicity" is a movement that started in 1981. Participants have committed to reducing the clutter, financial drain, job stress, and other areas of their lives that are keeping them from having what they consider to be most important—time with loved ones and connection with their community.[1]

Does this mean doing without or taking a vow of poverty? Not at all. It just means finding joy in what you have, doing with less, living within your means, and reconnecting with your family, friends, and community. It means living a more balanced, as well as a healthier, life. Research has shown that people in high-stress jobs have blood pressure approximately ten points higher than those in less stressful jobs. Studies have also shown that "people with a high ratio of credit card debt to income were in worse physical health than those with less debt."[2]

The mental health community recognizes the toll stress can have on mental and emotional health. Studies have shown that reducing stress and simplifying can help alleviate such tension-related disorders as insomnia, anxiety, muscle spasms, fatigue, and headaches.[3]

Let's look at some of the major areas that could be causing you difficulty and make some simple suggestions that might help you move toward simplification.

Stuff. If you're like many Americans, you probably own too many things. Advertisers get rich perpetuating the false notion that "keeping up with the Joneses" will help you feel better about yourself and more important. There's a grassroots movement called the "100 things challenge," where people have purposed to pare down their possessions to 100 things.[4] Impossible, you say? Perhaps. Maybe all you really want is to rid your kitchen counter of clutter. However, like those who are taking the challenge, start by making a list of what is absolutely necessary to your daily survival (clothes, kitchen items, furniture, etc.) and what you really could live without (clothes that no longer fit or are out of style, kitchen items that are broken or you don't use, furniture that is filling up your house and really isn't necessary) and then have a garage sale. Better yet, get your neighbors involved in the challenge and have a neighborhood garage sale. Use the proceeds to have a party. Learn to live the four R's—reduce, reuse, recycle, repair.

Electronics. Set boundaries on your electronics. Yes, you can actually turn off your cell phone at a reasonable hour and shut off your Internet and not check your e-mails after a certain time or even all weekend. "Researchers at Stanford University have found that the light from your computer monitor right before bed resets your whole wake/sleep cycle and can postpone the onset of necessary sleep by three hours. Constant cell phone use can keep you in an artificial sense of urgency, never allowing stress hormones and adrenaline to return to normal levels."[5] The TV also fits into this category and should be shut off an hour before bedtime. Information overload can be a cause of stress. With all the extra time you will have once you have these gadgets under control, you could play a game with your children or spouse or go take a walk. You'll be happier and healthier if you do.

Job. While not many of us have the luxury of quitting our jobs, there are ways to take control over the time you spend working. According to a Canadian Health Report quoted in *Reader's Digest*, "More than half of all employees take work home, 69 percent check their work e-mail from home, 59 percent check voice mail after hours, 30 percent get work-related faxes, and 29 percent keep their cell phones on day and night. Forty-six percent feel this work-related intrusion is a stressor, and 44 percent report 'negative spill-over' onto their families."[7] If these statistics describe you, it's time to set boundaries and keep a balanced perspective on your job. Leave it at the appointed time, don't let work carry over into the weekend, and spend the extra time with those you love, getting some exercise and doing something enjoyable and fun.

Finances/debt. Make a reasonable financial plan and stick to it. Purpose to live within your means, paying cash as often as you can. Hire a financial planner, if you can, who will show you how to pay off your credit card debt, start saving, and put some money away for retirement.

People. Yes, people can cause stress, especially those who are toxic or negative. Some people you may not be able to completely avoid, but you can limit your time with them and set boundaries on your emotions. "My mother is probably one of the most toxic people I know," said Jane. "After years of dealing with her anger, negativity, and not speaking to me for months over some perceived slight, I finally got up the nerve to tell her that I would no longer allow her to affect me and my family with her negativity and crazy making. Although I still see her, when she starts in on me, I tell her to stop or that I will leave."

Simplifying your life can be a difficult task, but you can do it . . . one step at a time. Once you have the momentum, you'll find yourself tackling areas you previously thought were impossible to change.

IF YOU WANT TO FEEL GREAT TODAY . . .

Start simple. Take one area and work to simplify that one part of your life this month. You will notice something amazing—you'll have more rewards from less. Honestly evaluate your life for signs of "too many" and "too much." Realize that your lack of simplicity may be robbing you of joy and peace. Examine these areas and set boundaries: stuff, electronics, job, finances, or even people.

34

Put Tele-Working to Work

There's a sense that people who telecommute are more flexible. . . . They can combine their home and work life, and they will go the extra yard when needed because they've been given the opportunity to better manage their time.

— Dana Gardner, analyst

I T'S MONDAY MORNING AND THE ALARM RUDELY awakens you from a sound sleep. You can do one of two things. You could reach over and turn it off, then crawl out of bed and into the shower, grab "breakfast" at a fast food establishment, then head across town to the office. Or you could do what millions of others are doing: shut off that alarm, catch another hour of sleep, then grab a healthy breakfast and head across the hall in your pajamas to work from your home office.

In his book *Microtrends*, Mark Penn noted that at that point 4.2 million Americans were working exclusively from home (a nearly 100 percent increase since 1990), while another 20 million worked from home part-time. Some were employees who telecommuted to traditional offices, but many more were independent: self-employed professionals, independent contractors,

editors, writers, or designers. Some were part-time or temporary workers for agencies that find and assign work to qualified
individuals able to complete the work at home.[1]

"Telecommuting is an arrangement by which people work at
home using a computer and telephone, transmitting work material to a business office. Although the term telecommuting was
coined in the early 1970s, the practice became more popular in
the 1990s as personal computers became more affordable and
the Internet became more accessible. Government agencies and
environmental groups encourage telecommuting because it reduces pollution, saves gasoline, and creates a less congested
commuting environment. Companies use telecommuting as a
way of keeping valued employees who might otherwise be lost
due to relocation or commuting stress. Some people feel they
can be more productive when working at home, while others
prefer an office environment."[2]

It was recently estimated that at least 3.9 million company
workers telecommute at least one day per week, saving a significant amount of gas ordinarily used in commuting to an office
while also reducing carbon dioxide emissions. It seems likely
that in the future more environmentally conscious companies
whose office workers conduct most of their work electronically
will not only allow but encourage their workers to work from
home, either part time or full time. And it isn't too far-fetched
to envision many future corporations conducting most if not all
of their business through employees living anywhere in the
world, their work connected via the Internet. Such "virtual"
companies will be able to accomplish as much work as they do
now, if not more, and their workers will surely be more satisfied
with their working situations, which may allow them to work
far more efficiently and creatively day by day since they don't
have to fight any traffic and they can work when they are most
productive or creative. Tele-working in this sense can include

private meetings held via the Internet, requiring fairly inexpensive audio and video equipment, with the net effect of reducing a company's costs for travel while increasing the individual worker's availability for work versus time spent traveling.

Home-based businesses are also increasing dramatically in number. These can include independent contracting, such as medical billing or editing. Other home-based work includes writing and other creative activities such as sculpture or painting or even house design. Dave knows one paraplegic who makes his living custom designing homes from the comfort of his own home office. The benefits of working at home include the lower costs and greater efficiency cited already in addition to certain tax-related benefits of using part of your home as your primary workplace.

Some home-based opportunities are really "pyramid schemes" in which one benefits from sharing the opportunity to share the opportunity. Fees are paid by new recruits and distributed "upward" to those who are developing the business, yet no real goods or services are distributed and no real "work" is done. Pyramid schemes are illegal in most developed countries, including the United States.

Network marketing opportunities are different in that a person joins a group of independent distributors of goods or services after being recruited, trained, and often provisioned by a "sponsor" who is already involved. Compensation is shared between the distributor and his or her "upline" according to the company's formula. Since multiple parties share the compensation, these endeavors are sometimes called multi-level marketing companies (MLMs). Some such companies seem to encourage using people to achieve one's own needs or goals. However, not all network marketing companies have such a philosophy. If you find the right one, it can be a "perfect match" as your business grows. Studying the differences before you sign the application can make all the difference in the world.

A few years ago, Richard Russell published an article in his Dow Theory Letters which he says has been the most popular, most widely requested, and most widely quoted piece he's ever written. In the article "The Perfect Business," Russell listed twelve characteristics of the ideal business. (Keep in mind that this was originally written before personal computers and the Internet, which is perhaps why he's updated the article twice.[3] To summarize Russell's list, the ideal business has a global market, offers something that people will buy even when finances are limited, offers a product that is proprietary (i.e. others cannot copy it), requires only a small number of employees, has low overhead, requires small up-front investment, operates on a cash basis, is minimally subject to government interference or regulation, is portable, is enjoyable, allows you to set your own pace, and provides residual income, even if you are not able to work or are on vacation.

You may think that no such business exists, but in this computer age, when the entire world is an Internet message away, it is possible to develop your own home-based business with the characteristics described above.[4]

IF YOU WANT TO FEEL GREAT TODAY . . .

Examine your job; see if you can replace any office time with telecommuting from home. Show your supervisor how this could make your work more effective and efficient. Looking for a new job? See where you could fit in as more businesses "outsource" tasks.

35

Go Where the
Wild Things Are

Live out loud and in full color.

– USA Olympian Jeff Olson

ONE SOURCE OF BOREDOM, DISAPPOINTMENT
or discontentment with life isn't so much that things
are going badly. The true source of the disappointment
is knowing deep inside that we have settled for "good enough"
versus being truly alive or, as some people put it, "living out loud."

One of Dave's closest friends is former downhill skier Jeff
Olson, a two-time Olympian, three-time U.S.A. champion, and
Pan Am Games gold medalist. Obviously Jeff has been more
than mediocre when it comes to athletics. However, as he's
gained wisdom with age, his focus has changed from first-place
finishes to family and faith, from victory to vitality. Several years
ago, he wrote the following reflections, slightly edited here:*

I live in a nice suburban home. A home with white walls
and white trim. Very white . . . too white. Antiseptic white.

You don't find that kind of white in nature.

John Eldredge wrote in his book *Wild at Heart*, "A man's soul cannot be suburbanized." When I read that passage, something stirred deep inside me. My heart roared with quiet desperation. Like a defiant prisoner of war, I knew deep down I was not meant for this antiseptic, "nice" domain.

Through God's grace, I discovered a wonderful book entitled *Romancing Your Child's Heart*. That book and its authors helped me realize that "suburbia" is a state of mind. Suburbia is middle class. Suburbia seduces you into comfortably numb living and parenting . . . "good enough" kind of living. It was a watershed moment for me. Deep inside, I knew that I was not meant to be a "suburban" (no pun intended) and just good enough. God had much bigger plans for me.

I am now on a grand "treasure hunt" with my children. Not a nice, clean Easter egg hunt at the local manicured golf course but an Indiana Jones kind of adventure . . . messy, crazy, dangerous, swashbuckling, roller coaster—an epic, mythic tale.

Eldredge also writes in his book, "Don't try to be 'nice' . . . do what makes you come alive . . . God needs more of those kind of people!" This notion is based on the fundamental premise that, at its core, the Christian heart is good. Therefore, it is okay to lean in to your passion . . . go with your gut . . . dust off your doldrums and come alive. You will bring glory to God, and your kids, if you have them, or others who see this change will join you.

I want my children to grow up living, breathing, and experiencing their Mom and Dad as fully alive. *Life is Beautiful*—remember that movie—regardless of the circumstances. True beauty breathes authenticity. If you have kids, would you rather have them say, "Dad's a really nice guy / Mom's a really hard worker" or "Dad rocks / Mom's got game . . . They really inspire me"?

Let's face it—there's enough darkness and dreariness all

around. It beats us down and beats us up. Tempts us to revert to the mean, the average, the good enough. But good enough is not good enough. I want to find the "shire" in life . . . that incredible lightness of being that comes with God's grace. My vision of heaven is like the hobbits' shire [in *The Lord of the Rings*] . . . a green, lush wonderland full of wonder and adventure and color and kinship.

So there I was, one summer morning, looking at my pathetic white suburban walls . . . watching my kids play with their numbing, plastic, unimaginative, non-toxic, non-flammable toys . . . and I got an idea. "We're going out," I said to my three beautiful young daughters.

"Daddy, noooooo . . . we're playing with our toys," they protested.

"You want toys," I said. "Wait till you see the toys God made for us. . . . Let's go."

After much whining and moaning and creative wooing, they acquiesced. Daddy might be going crazy, but they were getting to go along—cool.

"We're going to get wet," I warned. So we put on our adventure tennis shoes and set off to where the wild things are . . . in our case that would be Bear Creek that runs alongside our subdivision. There is a paved bike trail alongside Bear Creek. We have been on the path hundreds of times, walked down to the water's edge many times. But we had never ventured off the path, offshore, and into the creek—"the road less traveled."

At first my girls wouldn't go in. They didn't want to get their shoes wet. They had never done that on purpose before. "Dad . . . no way, we'll get wet!" they pleaded.

"Yahooooo! Exactly! Come on in . . . the water's great!" I cheered as I sat down in the middle of the creek. I was alive! I was going to get my nice, clean little girls muddy. But I couldn't force it. My youngest daughter, Siena, had wanted to come in before she started thinking. She hesitated after she observed her older sisters' faces (suburbia boxing their spirits in). My oldest daughter, Annecy, ventured in slowly, measuredly, and then squealed with rookie delight. Siena followed her in with innocence and joy restored.

I had to strike a deal with my stubborn daughter, Bella. I promised that if she came in, she could push me over in the creek. Her face lit up, expressing "I'm in for that!" She instantly forgot about the shoes and was with us moments later savoring the deal. As I fell backward, pushed with full exuberance, I saw her come alive, fully alive, along with the rest of us.

We set off upstream, taking turns as "leader," forging our way around bends and into the unknown—on high alert for new things, wild things, slimy things, special things, God things . . . his fingerprints. We laughed, we listened, we touched, we smelled, we saw, we splashed, we absorbed it.

Even the ordinary can be extraordinary when you're in awe. Finding God's grace and fingerprints right before your eyes makes any parent—no, any person—young at heart. And being young at heart makes all things new and every day great.

IF YOU WANT TO FEEL GREAT TODAY . . .

You must define "you," because you are more and bigger than the "box" that defines you, and has most likely been imposed on you by others. Break free, beyond your bounds. Add some zest to your life. Follow Jeff Olson's example and explore God's "toys" with your children, if you have children. Do it by yourself, if you don't. Read books like *Wild At Heart* and *Romancing Your Child's Heart* for innovative and energizing ideas, then turn the best ideas into action.

Become Not Like
the Tin Man

I must be right. Never an aspirin. Never injured a day in my life. The whole country, the whole world, should be doing my exercises. They'd be happier. — *Joseph H. Pilates, MD*

W HEN YOU WAKE UP FEELING ACHY AND stiff, stretching is one way to turn your day around. Too few of us realize what an important part stretching plays on our journey into fitness. We may be diligent about cardiovascular exercise and maybe even lift weights a few times a week, but stretching? Isn't that something cats and babies do?

Our often tense workdays may be spent sitting at a computer or even standing while performing a skill or activity. We do not give our bodies a chance to readjust; consequently, strain is repetitively placed on our joints and muscles. Our bodies are slumped and our shoulders are stooped, making it difficult even to breathe correctly. Poor posture becomes an unwelcome habit. It makes us look years older and can rob us of our zest for life. When our body deteriorates into a poorly run machine, it is like trying to take a drive on a beautiful day behind the wheel of a neglected car that spoils our fun by constantly breaking down. We soon lose our trust in our "vehicle" and will think twice about a repeat outing! A well-running body is a priceless treasure, so it is wise to do all we can to ensure proper maintenance.

As we age, our muscles and joints tighten up and can begin to restrict our range of motion. Just the normal process of aging alone can rob us of 20 to 30 percent of our muscle power. We discover reaching to the top shelf is not as easy as it once was, or bending to put on socks or getting in and out of the car is a bit of a chore. Knee joints that resist straightening can begin to cause a shuffling gait. We fear turning into the Tin Man and wonder if it is just a consequence of aging or if there is a way to turn it around. We have good news for you. The secret is to keep moving, thereby exercising our joints and stretching and building up the muscles that support them.

A review of the research on stretching by Ian Shrier, MD, PhD, and Kav Gossal, MD, was reported in *The Physician and Sportsmedicine*. The authors analyzed the benefits of stretching and concluded that stretching throughout the day is a means to increasing muscle size and strength. And, very importantly, inflexibility can be prevented and flexibility can be at least partially restored by stretching. Studies have shown that just a ten-week stretching program can produce improved performance in tests for speed, strength, power, and muscle endurance.[1]

A normal healthy joint has a rich blood supply flowing into the joint capsule which ensures smooth, painless movement of the joints. When the joint moves freely, the muscles surrounding the joint stay limber and slide easily along one another. Proper stretching not only feels wonderful but will go a long way toward keeping your body flexible and tuned up. You will discover that stretching is painless, needs no equipment, is free, and is easy to learn!

Jill had been a runner for most of her adult life, but at age fifty-five had to stop due to arthritis. At the same time, she changed jobs and went from being an active nurse on a busy orthopedic ward to a management position. She was enjoying her new job and gave little thought to her sudden change in activity level until she began to notice some disturbing changes. Back pain plagued her, and stiff knees made her unconsciously try to avoid the stairs. A stiff neck at the end of the day was her companion on the ride home from work. Jill had lost her vim and vigor and knew she needed help.

After some tests, her family doctor recommended that she join a health club and work with a personal trainer for a few sessions to get into a routine to try to turn around her muscle tension and painful joints. Jill was surprised to learn during her assessment with the trainer that she was on the road to permanent limitations in movement if she didn't begin muscle strengthening and, very importantly, stretching. Thankful that it was not too late to get preventative help, she followed the recommendations to the letter and was soon a familiar face at the health club on her way home from work. She learned the proper technique for stretching her tight muscles and was surprised that, after several weeks of diligence, her joint pain began to diminish. An added bonus was that she slept more soundly at night.

Stretching is known to provide these benefits:

- increased energy levels
- reduced muscle tension and soreness
- improved range of motion
- enhanced coordination
- improved posture and balance
- stimulated circulation
- augmented relaxation

Stretching should become a part of our everyday routine to help us maintain an active lifestyle. Stretching has many benefits, but a word of caution is necessary. Muscles are like taffy, and as any candy connoisseur knows, if you stretch cold taffy it may break. Therefore it is very important to warm up for at least five to ten minutes before you begin any stretching routine. It is also wise to get some good instruction before you begin. This will not only make stretching safe for you but also allow you to target the muscles and joints that are most in need of work. Many people enjoy water aerobics, yoga, or Pilates to meet their stretching quota. With guidance, you will not risk strengthening only part of a muscle group, which would rob you of some of the benefit. Your muscles were designed to work cooperatively as you go about your daily activities. Any physical therapist will assure you that it is much easier to maintain good range of motion than to attempt to rebuild it after problems arise.

Keep these guidelines in mind as you begin a stretching program: target your major muscle groups, always stay pain free, work up to holding each stretch for thirty seconds, no bouncing, don't forget to relax, and breathe deeply. Take a cue from your cat as it wakes from a nap, and thoroughly enjoy your time of stretching. It just could turn your day into a great one!

IF YOU WANT TO FEEL GREAT TODAY . . .

Stretch! This is exercise you can do all your life. It helps keep your body from breaking down, restricting movement. Stretching improves coordination, energy, circulation, and balance. Stretch every day and you'll notice less muscle tension and improved posture.

.... **37** ....

Stop Fixin' to do Something

Nothing is so fatiguing as the eternal hanging on of an uncompleted task.
— *William James*

YOU'VE STARED AT THE SAME TO-DO LIST FOR a week, wondering how in the world you're going to get it done. You've been putting out fires all week without getting to any of the things you wanted to do. What happens when you look at that list? Do you feel better? No, you probably feel guilty, depressed, overcommitted, overwhelmed, immobilized, or even like a failure for losing control of what is important to you—your life.

We often create lists because we feel overwhelmed and unorganized, hoping that at least making a list will help us. But few of us use those lists effectively. "There's a right way and a wrong way to do a to-do list," wrote Kathleen McGowan in *Psychology Today*. "According to procrastination researcher Timothy Pychyl, PhD, a professor of psychology at Carleton University in Ottawa, Canada, people often draw up a to-do list—and then rest on their laurels. The list itself becomes the day's achievement, allowing us to feel we've done something useful without taking on any real work. In fact, drawing up the list becomes a way of avoiding the work itself! Too often, the list is seen as the accomplishment for the day, reducing the immediate guilt of not working on the tasks at hand by investing energy in the list. When a list is used like this, it is simply another way in which we lie to ourselves."[1]

McGowan adds that Pychyl calls this the "procrastination field—we're preparing ourselves to work, we're getting all set to take it on, but we never actually start doing it. Instead, we waste time and make ourselves feel terrible by circling around it. For many people, that takes the form of attending to a barrage of tiny details and immediate requests. Burying yourself in busy-work is an effective way to avoid more important—and more challenging—tasks. Pychyl says that procrastinators typically 'binge' on low-priority activities, bustling about with stuff that's second- or third-level priority, rather than tackling the things they really need to do."[2]

Are you a true procrastinator—one of the 20 percent of all Americans—or are you just overbooked with too many deadlines and too much on your plate and just not sure how to tackle that list and get started? For true procrastinators, there seems to be a permanent gap between intention and action. In the South, these would be people who are "fixin' to do something" but can't ever seem to get to it. Procrastination involves putting something off because it is a task you just don't like doing—such as organizing your paperwork—and usually involves negative feelings such as guilt or anxiety. True procrastinators actively look for distractions and mentally try to figure out how to put something off, making excuses for not getting to a project. It's easier to check e-mail than to pay those bills, write that paper, and so on. It's a lifestyle, affecting every area of a procrastinator's life.[3]

Jenny is a busy single mom with four teenagers and a full-time job. She finds it helpful to make lists. However, when she can't get to everything on her list, she gets frustrated. She's good at prioritizing in most areas except when it comes to organizing her paperwork. "I don't know how to organize my files," she said. "When papers come in I put them where I think they should belong and then I can never find them again. My system is 'visual filing'—if I can see it, I take care of it. I hate doing paperwork and put it off as long as I can. When I do take the time to do it, I feel such a sense of relief and accomplishment that it's done. However, I don't keep it up, and within a short time I'm right back in a mess again."

Kyle is a busy songwriter and creative genius who runs a small nonprofit ministry. He's good at what he does, but he struggles with organization and puts off cleaning his office until he can't find anything. When he shuts off the phone and the computer and tackles the mess, he gets a lot done. "I feel so much better when I know where things are and the paperwork is manageable. Working off one list and not a hundred different pieces of paper is very helpful. I just wish I could keep it this way."

If you relate to Jenny and Kyle, here are some practical ideas to help you prioritize and reduce that to-do list:

- Tackle that one dreaded chore that stays on the top of your list for a while, or decide you're not going to do it, and take it off your list.
- Prioritize your list and assign numbers to the tasks—most important to least important. Break those items down into smaller, bite-sized pieces and do one piece at a time. Make an action plan to get them done. Windows need washing? Do the inside first, one room at a time, and then start on the outside. It may take you a week or two, but those windows will get cleaned.
- Schedule alternating tasks: spend one hour on a number one priority item, and then reward yourself by doing something easier that's a lower priority for the next thirty min-

utes. Finish that, and cross it off.

- Use "dead" time to your advantage. For example, if you have an appointment where you know you'll be waiting, write a letter while you're waiting, pay some bills, finish reading that overdue library book. Learning to use your time more efficiently will help you in the long run.
- Keep your focus. Do you ever feel like you're trying to do fifty things at once? When doing a priority item, keep a notepad with you and jot down other things that come to mind. Do those when you have finished the project you are working on.
- Get realistic about what you have to do and the amount of time you have. Don't beat yourself up because you can't get it all done immediately, because realistically, you probably can't. Focus on the best use of your time now.[4]

And, finally, remember to reward yourself after the completion of a task and a job well done. There's nothing like sitting in your favorite chair with your favorite beverage looking at those clean windows and crossing that item off your list.

IF YOU WANT TO FEEL GREAT TODAY . . .

Decide you no longer want to be controlled by your long-outdated "to-do" list, and start a new one using the suggestions in this chapter. If something must be done, take baby steps. Each small step takes you closer to the goal. If you are a "true" procrastinator, you might consider seeking professional help to change your thinking processes in this area.

38

Unearth Those Skeletons

Why waste your money looking up your family tree? Just go into politics and your opponents will do it for you!
                                                                    – Mark Twain

I N JUST ABOUT EVERY FAMILY TREE THERE ARE
ancestors we are proud of and those we don't want to claim
as relatives. While it would be fun to claim Abraham Lincoln as an ancestor, we probably wouldn't want to admit we are related to John Wilkes Booth—even if our last name is Booth.

Once reserved for the "royals and rulers," genealogy has become a popular pastime and hobby for anyone who is interested in their family history. Alex Haley's 1970s movie *Roots: The Saga of an American Family* caused a surge in the popularity of genealogy as a hobby. With the availability of the Internet, the number of resources has increased, which has made genealogical information readily accessible.[1]

Allison Merline writes, "The motivation to conduct genealogical research varies from religious belief systems, pride of descent from certain groups, the desire to know medical and family history of an adopted individual, or celebrating resilience of families who survived poverty or slavery."[2] Some families are even proud to claim those not-so-socially-acceptable "skeletons in the closet" as part of their heritage and as something that has contributed to who they are today.

Besides being fun, genealogy has health benefits. Adrienne Horne, a master's student in anthropology at the University of Calgary, researched what motivates people to trace their ancestry and what keeps them committed to it. She found that although a lot of information is available on how to study a family history, very little information exists on who is involved, why people do it, and what benefits it offers.[3]

When questioning the people in her study, Horne found that many got involved because they were never told stories about their families. They were interested in learning about their heritage and even in uncovering family secrets. Those involved tended to be very social. The act of researching and compiling information gave them a sense of accomplishment. Horne cites other benefits as well: "tracing family heritage helps older people deal with death and accept their own mortality," and, although most families find their ancestors were just ordinary people and not at all famous, genealogy gives the researcher a sense of worth and belonging.[4]

Lester Hartrick discusses additional psychological benefits of studying genealogy and states, "By studying the lives and times of our ancestors, we are broadened by the knowledge gained. Finally the study of our progenitors can provide us with insight into their personal lives. With this knowledge we are better able to understand ourselves, for it is they who at least in part have determined who we are."[5] He reports that by studying his own family history, he has found belonging, acceptance, friendship, and a love for the many new friends and family he has found while pursuing this hobby. He considers it a privilege to see and know his ancestors for the real living people they were, finding that they had some of the same joys and failures that we experience today, only in the context of their lives at the time.

Sue became interested in genealogy several years ago, mostly due to her mother's interest and research. "If you like detective work and gain satisfaction in uncovering new information, you could easily become a genealogy junky," she said. "I did. I found it fascinating to find relatives who had come to the New World from Scotland and to see what contributions they made to the world around them. I found relatives my mother didn't know about. In fact, it was while researching her family that I found a first cousin in Texas, unbeknownst to my mother. Nancy has since become an important part of our family and is a valuable family historian."

Nancy writes, "I began genealogy research on my paternal family shortly after my father died in 1997. I did a search for my maiden name and came up with a long list of potential relatives nationwide. I sent an e-mail to everyone on the list, and one man put me in touch with several relatives in Texas, where I live. My father had always said that we had no local relatives. After attending a family reunion, I met relatives who live within twenty minutes of my home.

"Genealogy research allows plenty of room for an escape into a sort of fictional reality world," she added, "an opportunity to write a book in my imagination, although what I actually know is just information. I sometimes find myself in the stories I read and wonder if I could have lived like they did. Knowing more about my family history fosters a feeling of wholeness. My life and values were molded, in part, by my ancestors' experiences, choices, and philosophies that have trickled down the generations. Genealogy has personalized history for me, and I feel in touch with my past and my today."

How do you get started on the journey to finding more about your past, which may lead to a better understanding of your today? You might start by gathering information from family members. If you're fortunate, someone will have been a historian. Do an Internet search on your last name or other family names. Chances are that others have researched their own relatives who are connected to yours in some way, and, through their work, you can learn more about your own family. There are many genealogical message boards where you can post questions about ancestors and family members, which is how Sue found Nancy. Do an Internet search for genealogy web sites. You will find several, some of which are free and others which require membership. The public library is another good source of information; some cities even have genealogy libraries.

Have fun, meet some new relatives, and find out about some old ones. Just remember, however, that if you'd rather spend time in a library than a shopping mall, you've probably become addicted to genealogy.

IF YOU WANT TO FEEL GREAT TODAY . . .

Keep in mind that as you discover your family's history and lineage—be it good, bad, or ugly—the most important family ties for believers is that they're children of the King. If you discover some "skeletons" in your family's genealogical closet, do not be dismayed, but be thankful that your own good reputation shows that poor choicemaking is not genetic. Every family needs a historian, so if you have an interest in genealogy in general, and your family's roots in particular, perhaps you're the one to catalogue the past for future generations.

.... **39** ....

Rock On, Groove to the Beat, or Hum with a Hymn

Take a music bath once or twice a week for a few seasons. You
will find it is to the soul what a water bath is to the body.[1]
— *Oliver Wendell Holmes*

F OR MOST OF US, LIFE WITHOUT MUSIC WOULD
be unthinkable. We've grown up with music in one form
or another and have learned to enjoy a variety of sounds—
from a classical Mozart or Beethoven to country, jazz, easy listening, gospel, or perhaps even rap or rock and roll. From those
simple nursery rhymes and lullabies we learned as children,
we've developed a more sophisticated palate, and we have definite likes or dislikes in the music we listen to. Sometimes those
tastes vary depending on our moods and the seasons in our lives.

God created us to respond innately to anything with rhythm.
Our bodies are naturally rhythmic. Take a moment to think
about the natural rhythm of your heartbeat and listen to your
own breathing. Reflect on how your internal organs work per-
fectly together just like a well-orchestrated symphony. Your ears

are constructed to hear different kinds of sounds. Your body responds to the rhythm in music. Notice how your foot almost automatically taps to the rhythm when certain kinds of music are played. Children, who are naturally uninhibited, will get up and dance to a lively tune.

Music has the ability to transport us back to our past. Hearing a certain song can often evoke memories of happy or sad times. Remember your first love and that special song you had? Music also affects our present moods and emotions in ways that mere words alone cannot do. It is a well-known fact that music has healing qualities, helping us find healing for hurt, sadness, pain, and other emotions that we tend to keep bottled up. Music also transports us into the future. Gospel music is well known for its ability to provide hope for a better life ahead. Music keeps us young, vibrant, and alive.

"Young at Heart," an octogenarian singing group from New England, has found that music is keeping them young and active and providing the incentive and motivation to enjoy life and keep going in spite of the issues seniors often face. Bob Cilman, choral director of "Young at Heart," reports that his choir members are basically stress free (something he himself cannot lay claim to). Stan Goldman, one of the choir members, advises all of us to "keep moving, keep learning, and have fun."[1]

We know that music affects our moods—slow music can relax us, while something fast paced and upbeat can energize us. "Brain waves are modified by sounds. Music with about 60 beats per minute, such as that of Mozart, Brahms, and Bach, shifts the brain activity from Beta to higher-awareness Alpha waves, thus resulting in relaxed concentration. Known as the 'Mozart Effect,' this type of music lowers stress and increases concentration. A study in England found that students scored 10 points higher on an IQ test after listening to Mozart compared to those exposed to silence, white noise (low-level random sounds, such as radio static, running water, traffic, etc.), or other music."[2]

Have you ever paid attention to the music playing in the stores where you shop? What you are hearing is not random but is specifically designed to shape your behavior. "Music can be used to make people move faster or slower, to encourage them to shop longer, persuade them to action, or help them relax."[3] The next time you are shopping, listen to the music and see how it affects your mood and shopping behavior. Elevator music, also known as lift music, piped music, or Muzak "refers to the gentle instrumental arrangements of popular music designed for playing in shopping malls, grocery stores, department stores, public toilets, telephone systems (while the caller is on hold), cruise ships, airports, doctors' and dentists' offices, and elevators."[4]

Research seems to support the idea that music can help you become more productive at work. "A trial where 75 out of 256 workers at a large retail company were issued with personal stereos to wear at work for four weeks showed a 10 percent increase in productivity for the headphone wearers. Other similar research conducted by researchers at the University of Illinois found a 6.3 percent increase when compared with the no music control group."[5] Does it matter the type of music? According to the same article, music with a constant, easy beat and light melodies help increase concentration. Music with an upbeat rhythm has been shown to reduce stress hormones by as much as 41 percent.

Sharon, who has been singing for many years, said that "Music is rather like a pet. It doesn't ask questions. It's just there for you. The notes, the harmony are the same, no matter who is listening. When I need a good cry, I know what songs or types of music to play. When I need to stop feeling sorry for myself, ditto. If I need to exercise and don't want to. . . . Name it, and there is music or a song for it.

"Music forms bonds between people that nothing else can. The lullaby I sang for my children, the song that was playing the first time a boy asked me to dance, the specials my husband and I sing at church or as we ride along in the car—all of these moments are forever captured by, and connected to, a melody."

How do we best enhance the effects of music? One article stated, "The best way to de-stress yourself is to lie back with a pair of headphones and become part of the music. Select music that has a pace slower than 72 [beats] per minute. This will ease your heartbeat and relax you. Combine music with your morning walk and you will feel doubly rejuvenated by combining the goodness of exercise and music."[6]

Anna Lynn Sibal states that we can avail ourselves of the healing properties of music by putting it into our everyday lives. Most of us do this in some form anyway. She suggests starting our day with some upbeat music to wake ourselves up and prepare for the day ahead. On the commute to work, play your favorite CDs or MP3s, which can relieve you of the stress of dealing with traffic. Play soothing music at work or while doing chores. At mealtimes, soothing music can help us digest our food better. Listening to music as we try to get to sleep helps us get the rest we need.[7]

Whatever genre you choose to listen to, music can simply help you to feel great.

IF YOU WANT TO FEEL GREAT TODAY . . .

Whether you rock on, groove to the beat, or hum with a hymn, music is there to move you. Rejuvenate your internal world by surrounding your soul with music. Listen to a variety of types of music to see what really resonates with you. Observe how music affects you and those around you. Enjoy it as the divine gift that it is.

40

Hang Ten!

Dogsled-riding is a sport that is relaxing as well as fragrant.
                                                          – Dave Barry

I T'S EASY TO FORGET HOW INVIGORATING IT CAN be to try something new. Researchers suggest that if we are brave enough to get out there and try a new sport or activity, we will be rewarded with a lot of fun as well as a stronger body and sharper brain.

Research conducted by the University of Chicago found that playing, and even watching, sports improves brain function by changing the neural networks in the brain. The areas involved in comprehension tap into the areas that are activated when we actually perform sports skills.[1] So no more excuses! Trying a new sport is good for the body and the mind. It can even be good for your spirit.

Stan, a friend of ours, had always wanted to try dogsledding. He admired the husky breed that loves to race across the snow, pulling a sled of adventurers. God took extra time when he created huskies with their brilliant blue eyes peering out from beneath their downy gray fur coat. He infused them with an insatiable desire to pull, and pull they will, the moment they are called to duty! Powerful legs equip them to lug heavy loads quite effortlessly.

One spectacular winter day, Stan decided he had waited long enough and called an adventurous buddy and signed them up for their first dogsled trek. "The sky was that surreal cornflower blue and the air clear and crisp after the snowfall had blanketed the ridge high up in the Colorado mountains," he recalls. "The walk up to the dogsled camp was a spiritual experience I won't forget. Snow-laden firs sparkled in the sunlight and directed my thoughts toward our Creator as the words of that great hymn 'How Great Thou Art' ran through my mind:

> When through the woods and forest glades I wander,
> And hear the birds sing sweetly in the trees;
> When I look down from lofty mountain grandeur
> And hear the brook and feel the gentle breeze.
> Then sings my soul, my Savior God, to Thee:
> How great Thou art, how great Thou art![2]

"Crunching along the path and through the snow, we could hear the huskies baying in the distance and, as we rounded the corner, saw the majestic dogs nestled in the snow along their tether line. These friendly people-lovers greeted us warmly. Our guide signed us up and took us through the safety maneuvers, and four of us first-timers were loaded into the sled beneath fur blankets. One by one the dogs were greeted warmly by name and hooked to their harnesses in front of our sled. Their exuberance was catching as each dog vied for a turn with yelps and pleading eyes. They clearly love their job! Then came the classic call of 'mush,' and we lurched forward, speeding across the snowy ridge. I was shocked by our roller-coaster speed and the power of our dog team as they whisked us around the first curve. The view was breathtaking from the top of the ridge, and we could see the Continental Divide in the distance. 'Hang on!' the guide shouted out as he let the brake out all the way, and we were flying over the knolls, across streams, skillfully dodging trees! I was in heaven—and reminded of the awesome handiwork of its primary Resident. Too soon we rounded the corner and slowed as we headed back to camp ready to sign up for one more spin. I realized with a laugh that the sport of dogsledding had captured me with the same intensity as my first toboggan ride at age six!"

While working in Hawaii, I (Jim) was mesmerized as I watched the expert surfers on the famed North Shore skillfully and effortlessly navigate the huge twenty- to thirty-foot waves. Not being the Walter Mitty type, I knew for certain that these huge waves would forever be a spectator sport for me. But I thought: How hard can it be to surf the smaller, tranquil ones on the South Shore?

After getting in the mood by buying a surfing T-shirt, my son tipped the balance with a birthday surf-lesson certificate. I was ready to go for it and scheduled my lesson in the calm waters off Waikiki Beach. The big day finally arrived, but I noticed as we walked down the beach that the waves were not as small as I remembered. With some trepidation I lined up with the group of much younger students for the "dry land" portion of the lesson. I knew I was in trouble from the start as my arms just didn't seem long enough to allow my entire body to push up into the proper "hang ten" position on my long board. The instructor, ever the optimist, insisted I would do just fine once I was in the water. Before I knew it, I was paddling my way out into the waves with the other students. My first impression was that these were the biggest waves I had ever seen up close! My first attempt to stand resulted in a spectacular backward flip off my surfboard.

To make a long story short, the surf was "up" much more than I was! I survived the lesson with a few bruises but had the satisfaction of trying a new sport and basking in the thrill of at least once in my life being propelled full speed across the ocean on a gigantic wave. Such an experience with the power and majesty of a giant wave is surely a reminder of how powerful and majestic our wave Maker is!

So are you ready to leave the sidelines and try your hand at something you have always wanted to do? It can be tame and elegant like ice skating or bold and a bit risky like downhill skiing. Or you could join the many Americans who love table tennis, golf, bike riding, or race walking. Whatever you decide, you are guaranteed to have a great day and—who knows?—you may even get hooked like our friend Stan.

IF YOU WANT TO FEEL GREAT TODAY . . .

Don't think too much about this one. Just do it! Get out there and try something new. Be adventurous and invigorate your body, mind, and spirit with a new sport. No, you're not too old. You're never too old to try something you have always wanted to do. But if there's any danger, arrange for an expert to train and possibly even go with you . . . whether it's surfing, snow skiing, rock climbing, or skydiving. Remember when you learned to ride a bike as a kid? Maybe somebody or something steadied you for a while, but eventually you got the knack of it and off you went. Adopt that same mindset with that new sport you're a bit hesitant to try.

········· **41** ·········

Try a "Spice to Life" Meal

Spice is life. It depends upon what you like. . . . Have fun with it. Yes, food is serious, but you should have fun with it.
— Emeril Lagasse, TV chef

F OOD REALLY IS A SPICE OF LIFE. TO PROVE THIS, just ask someone about their most exotic meal. Most people have no trouble reaching back in their memories and providing a detailed account of some long-ago eating adventure. This is because strong emotion is a key ingredient to securely locking away memories. When people can passionately recall the details of that long-ago meal, it is a good bet that the meal or dish was an emotional event. It added a spice to their life. Food is powerful and capable of reaching our emotive core and altering our life experience and perception. A recent study on the connection between food and emotions found that food activates the hippocampus area of the brain on a PET scan. This is the area linked to memory, sensory and motor impulses, and emotional behavior.[1] So be aware that the selection of a mood-altering food is a tool at your disposal to avoid slipping into the blues. Waking up your taste buds could very well change your day.

Just to be clear, "spice to life" food is not comfort food, which has its own place in our arsenal of culinary tools for influencing our emotional and spiritual state. Comfort food helps many people when they are feeling sad or down. But if foods were like water sports, comfort food would be a dip in a tranquil pool while a spice to life food would be jet skiing in the Caribbean. You can love them both, but they're certainly not the same!

One of the most peculiar things about spice to life foods is that the experience does not even have to be pleasant. The food experience only has to be totally different and exotic. One traveler: "I was in South Korea and saw a street vendor who was frying up small nuts the size of pine nuts. I was hungry and ordered a paper cup of these nuts. They had a very peculiar flavor. Inspecting the nuts more closely as I walked along, I discovered they each had six little lines on them. I soon found out that those lines were actually what was left of the legs! I had been eating bugs. My spirits were immediately lifted as I had a good laugh at myself and a memorable story to tell for years to come."

Our friend Bruce recalls living in Hawaii: "I encountered all sorts of treats that were unfamiliar to my New England palate. Such treats are available everywhere in Hawaii. Some come from the Far East like li hing mui, a popular mixture of five spices. Others are more local like poi, made from taro leaves. I want to be sensitive toward other people's food preferences, but I do not know how else to say this. Everything in my New England being told me that some of these 'treats' were not actually meant to be food. However, these 'non-food products' raised my spirits considerably when I shared my food experiment stories at the office. Everyone became interested in what I had eaten and why I couldn't finish it! And then they told me their stories. Soon we started bringing in exotic foods to the office to see what else might elicit a rejection or delight."

Spice to life foods need not be inedible, but they should be exotic. If you live near an urban center, the choices abound. We recommend eating an ethnic food that is completely out of your normal range of dining choices. If you love Italian food, then try something from Bangladesh!

If you live in a rural setting, you may have to prepare your own exotic dish. The food must be starkly different and outside your normal range. We recommend aromatic foods prepared with spices like cilantro, coriander, ginger, lavender, nutmeg, oregano, sage, spearmint, or rosemary, to name a few that are commonly available. Exotic spices may be hard to acquire at a rural grocery store, but the Internet can be a great resource. You can order exotic ground spices and even look up recipes from around the world that have their own rich histories and stories.

Have the playful attitude that food doesn't always have to taste pleasant to provide a spice to life experience. Be bold in your selection. Don't ask, "Do I think I'll like it?" Instead ask, "Is this really different?" Share the meal with company. If dining out, invite a friend or someone you would like to know better. If dining in, it is best to only invite someone you already know and trust. After all, there is the real chance that the meal will not be pleasing to everyone's palate, and you don't want that to be anyone's first impression of your culinary skill!

IF YOU WANT TO FEEL GREAT TODAY . . .

When you need a monotony-breaking pick-me-up, plan to do some exotic dining. Invite a friend and enjoy the bold experience of unusual food. Try cuisine you normally shy away from. Choose dishes with aromatic spices. Food really adds a spice to life. Hello new food, and hello good mood!

42

Tune to the Maker's Channel

A man prayed, and at first he thought that prayer was talking. But he became more and more quiet until in the end he realized that prayer is listening. — Søren Kierkegaard

WHILE YOU WERE READING THAT QUOTE, an uncountable number of television and radio waves passed through your brain. But you didn't hear or see anything as a result because your brain wasn't properly equipped or tuned in to those channels.

Sometimes it's like that with our down times. We get so focused on one thing or another—our debts, problems, or challenges, for example—that all we "see" are the difficulties, and all we "hear" is background interference, the volume more or less controlled by our level of anxiety. Since we can only really consciously "tune in" to one thing at a time, is it any wonder that our own internal static can drown out the "still, small voice" of God (1 Kings 19:12), which can only be "heard" when we have a sense of calm, serenity, or inner quietness in our souls?

In addition to the "noise" that can come from within, our world bombards us with external noise, from blaring sounds to signs along the road saying, "You need me. I taste good. I can make you happy. I can make you rich. I am the answer to your deepest desires." In our modern world, you can go to the most remote place and still not find real silence due to aircraft of various kinds flying by overhead. I (Dave) recall how eerie it was on September 11, 2001, when the skies went silent. I didn't know why and hardly noticed at first. I was in camp in the Colorado Rockies, at about 10,000 feet in elevation, and so used to hearing airliners passing by periodically on their routes to and from Denver that it took awhile to realize that all of a sudden it had become a lot quieter than normal. Not long thereafter, I learned by cell phone what had happened, though from that vantage point it was hard to imagine.

If you sit on a park bench today and simply observe the people around you, you'll note that many of them are rollerblading or walking or just sitting while talking on their cell phones. Many others may be swaying to the noise emanating from the little earphones in their ears, hooked to their tiny MP3 players or Walkmans or, if they're old like us, transistor radios. And when they get home, the TV or stereo or computer will be on most of the rest of their waking hours, leaving very little time, if any, for silence.

I (Dave) will not be surprised if implants are available in the not-too-distant future to provide continual access to TV, phone, computer, or radio (or all of these and more) with the signal going directly to the brain. This might seem intriguing at first, but the net result for some would be just a step beyond what is available today, in that someone with this implant could live an entire day, month, year, or lifetime without ever having a single moment of silence. In terms of this chapter's topic, the net effect would be that every moment of every day would be filled with noise, with no opportunity to tune in to "the Maker's channel," which can only be achieved when everything else is turned off.

In his book *The Way of the Heart*, one of our favorite spiritual writers, the Roman Catholic priest Henri J. M. Nouwen, wrote, "When Arsenius, the Roman educator who exchanged his status and wealth for the solitude of the Egyptian desert, prayed, 'Lord, lead me into the way of salvation,' he heard a voice saying, 'Be silent.'"[1]

This exhoes a Psalm, penned by Israel's King David, a former shepherd, who had spent untold nights out under the stars, listening to the bleating of the sheep, and also to the "voice" of God: "My soul, wait in silence for God only, for my hope is from Him" (Ps. 62:5, NASB).

Anyone who has spent a lot of time outdoors knows, as David knew, that it is one of the best places to tune in to the Maker's channel. Birders, mushroomers, hikers, canoeists, kayakers, anglers, and other outdoors people know this. While many of them may only focus on their reason for being out there, some experience truly significant, wordless encounters with the Maker through what he made. Our friend Mike Brooks, who is the chief visionary officer for the Christian Outdoor Fellowship of America,[2] described one such experience in one of his stories:

> I was going through a hard time in my life and wondered if God was hearing my prayers. I poured out my soul to him. I let him know that I needed to hear from him. I wanted a sign, what I call "Jesus with real skin" to sit down and talk and listen to me, hear my heartaches, feel my pain, and comfort me. I was talking with him from a tree stand in an old poplar tree about twenty feet up. The sky was overcast, the wind blew, and the flurries began to fall. The tree rocked slightly and the cold wind was starting to go through my hunting coat; it was downright cold. The brown grass below me danced in the patches of snow that dotted the forest floor. I

bowed my head in prayer and asked for a sign from God.

As I opened my eyes I glanced down at the rifle sitting on my lap, and at the very end of the barrel was a wren! It looked at me with its head twitching from left to right. It hopped a little closer toward the stock. I was amazed at the courage of this little bird, but then it hit me that God had been with me all along, and this beautiful creation of God spoke of that fact louder than any human could. The surroundings became a living portrait of the One who made all this creation, and the answer to my pleadings became that little wren. This wren began to chirp and carry on. I'm not sure how long it sat on the barrel of my gun, but after it left, I sat in awe of God and really started thanking him for all he had blessed me with. It didn't take long before I was feeling better and had a better perspective on where I fit into my Maker's plan.

IF YOU WANT TO FEEL GREAT TODAY . . .

One of the best ways is to "tune in" to your Maker, who wants you to know that he is there and he understands and cares. The message may not come through a little bird, or a sunset or a sonnet, an orchid or an orchestra. But if you listen more than speak and seek more than strive, your entire outlook can be turned around. Take the time to be silent and listen for his voice. After you settle in and the cacophony of internal and external noise subsides, you may hear him whisper more of faith versus doubt, joy versus sorrow, peace instead of fear, hope instead of despair. "I am here," he whispers, still. "I am always here, and I will never leave you nor forsake you, for I am a friend who is closer than a brother to you."

43

Set Sail for New Adventures

When I get a little money, I buy books. And if there is any left over, I buy food. — *Deciderius Erasmus*

CURLING UP ON THE COUCH WITH A GOOD book, a fire in the fireplace, and a cup of your favorite beverage is a wonderful way to spend an afternoon, especially if it's raining or snowing outside. Whatever your preference in reading, reading good literature is a pastime that is good for you.

Reading can transport you out of your normal mindset and into a whole new realm of possibilities. It can take you to times and places and people that you otherwise might never know existed. Reading can provide an escape from the laundry, a sink full of dirty dishes, your problems at work, and anything else you'd like to forget for a while.

According to a recent survey by the National Endowment for the Arts, literary reading is increasing among adult Americans; specifically, 113 million adult Americans did some literary reading that year. The report, "Reading on the Rise," documents what it calls a "significant turning point in recent American cultural history. For the first time in over a quarter-century, our survey shows that literary reading has risen among adult Americans. After decades of declining trends, there has been a decisive and unambiguous increase among virtually every group measured in this comprehensive national survey."[1]

Activities such as reading that keep your brain intellectually stimulated and active have been shown to reduce the onset of dementia and Alzheimer's disease. This alone is a very good reason to unplug your gadgets and pick up a book and read for at least thirty minutes a day. Other advantages to reading include that it:

- improves your vocabulary by exposing you to new words
- improves concentration and focus as you process large chunks of information
- builds self-esteem by helping you become more knowledgeable
- improves memory—use it or lose it
- improves your discipline as you make time to read
- improves creativity by helping to develop the creative side of the brain
- gives you something to talk about by broadening your horizons of information
- reduces boredom by always giving you something to do.[2]

If you're not a reader, you can start by setting aside thirty minutes each day to read something, whether it's a magazine, book, newspaper, devotional book, Bible, or some other reading matter—such as this book, of course. Pick a quiet place in your house with a comfortable couch or chair. Many people like to read either in the early morning hours or right before bed. You'll soon find what works best for you.

If you're not sure of the kinds of things you'd like to read, spend some time looking over the selections at your local bookstore. Note what's on the best-seller list and look through some of those titles to see if they fit your taste.

As you get more involved in reading, you might visit your local library where books can be checked out at no charge. One advantage—if you don't like the book, you can return it and you are not out the cost. Most public libraries have their card catalog online, and this makes choosing and reserving books easy.

"I am a voracious reader," said Sue. "I love all kinds of books. However, many of the books I've read are ones that I would never read again. I have taken boxes of books to the local thrift store. When I lost my job, I knew I didn't want to stop reading, so I got a library card. I reserve a book online, and it is sent to my local branch where I pick it up. I love being able to read the latest books by my favorite authors when it doesn't cost me anything."

Another fun thing to do is to join a book club, which consists of a group of people who meet on a regular basis to discuss a book they have chosen to read prior to that meeting. Ask around. You are likely to find one or know someone who knows of one. Or start one yourself. This is a great way to broaden your reading interests while enjoying the social aspect of getting together with the other club members.

If you have children, read aloud to them. Children are especially prone to connect to the latest electronic gadget because that's what their friends do. Set aside time each night to read something that fits your child's age level and interest. You will be improving your own reading skills while improving your child's, plus helping to develop a love of reading in your child. When you choose a series that has been turned into movies, such as *The Chronicles of Narnia* or *The Lord of the Rings*, you can enjoy them with your children in a double sense and even compare the movies to the books for an added bonus. All you have to do is grab a book and set sail for new adventures—with your kids or just by yourself!

IF YOU WANT TO FEEL GREAT TODAY . . .

Read. Reading is a window to the world, which you get to see through someone else's eyes. When you have some leisure time, take a "trip." It's good for your brain. Open up a good book, and you are instantly pulled to another time and place, into a process of thinking or toward the acquisition of information that expands your perspective. When you find an insight you want to remember, write it in your personal book of quotes. When you discover a good book, put it on your list of titles to mention to friends and family or to share with your reading club.

········· **44** ·········

Go Surfing With No Board

The Internet is becoming the town square for the global village of tomorrow. — *Bill Gates*

W HEN DAVE WAS A STUDENT AT A PREP school in New Hampshire, his dorm had one phone, which everyone could use, knowing that anybody might overhear the conversation. The reason? It was a box on the wall with one of those little black mouthpieces sticking out about eight inches from the box, a separate handset for listening that looked a little like a short black flashlight, and a little handle on the side you had to turn to ring up the operator, who would plug in the wire to the world like Ernestine on "Laugh-In," played by Lily Tomlin. "One ringy-dingy, two ringy-dingies" . . . and maybe you could actually hear the party you were trying to reach and they, you. And the calls were not cheap, even back then when a quarter bought almost a gallon of gas.

Not too long ago, Dave was able to use Voice over Internet Protocol (VoIP) to do a three-way phone call including Dave (who was in Colorado at the time), his wife, who was in Poland, and Bobbie Dill, who was in Hawaii. The reception was perfect,

. . . .

and best of all, the call was free. Well, virtually free. There was no charge for the call itself to any of the parties because Dave was paying a monthly fee to Vonage for the VoIP access, which he used to call the others, after which he pushed the right buttons (for a change) and, voilà, all could chat across nearly half the globe.

In olden times, when you got stressed out, you ate some ice cream or chocolate or maybe took a bike ride or a long walk. Today there's the Internet. It's not an evil thing, as some may think. Its degree of good or evil is like that of a lot of other things—it depends on how you use it. Yes, the Internet has porn and online "dating" chat rooms you should avoid as well as a variety of other uses that are evil or sometimes even deadly, as seen in the story of the Florida teen who took his own life, pill by pill, as other participants online with him at that time egged him on. Selectivity is crucial, and protecting yourself and your family from malicious contacts or viruses that can ride into your computer on the back of just about anything is absolutely essential.

But millions use the Internet every day for enjoyment and relaxation. So here are a few examples and suggestions for how to proceed if you want to give it a try:

Join a forum that is sponsored and controlled by an organization you trust. There you can "meet" and converse with others with similar interests or experiences, share ideas and solutions if you have common issues, and even pray for one another, one digital byte after another. This is just one aspect of what is called "social networking," which the Internet has made a worldwide, instantaneous reality.

Find a game that you might enjoy playing, keeping in mind that some of the "games" available online are violent or filled with sexual innuendo, or worse. Several of our friends and family members recommended the following word games: Word

Whomp, Sudoku, Pathwords, and Scramble. In some cases, as with games on Facebook.com, you can practice solo until you are ready to "compete," then invite someone to play the same game with you. Sometimes whole groups of people can match wits with the game and each other simultaneously, each from the privacy of his or her own computer location. Caution: some have said that playing these games can be a bit addictive.

Establish your own blog. The word blog is a contraction of the term "web log." It describes an individual's web site, upon which you might find commentary, descriptions of events, or other material such as graphics or video. It's like an online diary that anyone can read and that is updated whenever you can do so. A "blogger" is someone who maintains a blog. "To blog" means to maintain or add to (or edit) your blog. Some blogs allow visitors to post comments or otherwise interact with what is on that blog. Best estimates are that there are now more than 200 million English language blogs. "With the advent of video blogging, the word blog has taken on an even looser meaning—that of any bit of media wherein the subject expresses his opinion or simply talks about something."[1]

Find and share humorous, wise, inspiring, or otherwise interesting audio or video. For videos check out YouTube.com. Dave's all-time favorite inspirational YouTube clip is the initial performance of Paul Potts, a UK cell-phone salesman who received a standing ovation the first time he sang on Britain's Got Talent, and who went on to win that year's competition. His beautiful singing will make you weep.[2]

Skype somebody. Skype.com has changed forever the horizons of high-speed Internet communication, both audio and video. The service is free when both parties are members (there is no membership charge, either). And, if you wish, you can make other calls to land lines or cell phones for a minimal cost. Skype uses the Voice over Internet Protocol in a broader way than most other services. Using this service you can, at no additional cost beyond the cost of the web camera (which can be less than $10, and is often built into laptops now), allow the person at the other end to see you—if they also have a web camera, of course. But what fun families separated by the miles can have when each party has a good web camera and a Skype account. Perhaps this is one reason that, as I write these words, 21,893,649 people are online with Skype.

Bobbie enjoys "Skyping" family and friends. "The first time our son told us about Skype, we were amazed that there was such an inexpensive and fun way to 'beam yourself' into the midst of your family's life thousands of miles away!" she wrote. "When everything was finally in place, we connected with a stroke of the keyboard and were miraculously face-to-face with our son. As any parent knows, there is no substitute for actually 'seeing' your son or daughter. The thrill was palpable. We basked in a half hour of free conversation, discussed plans for our next family get-together, and saw recent pictures he posted as we talked. When we finally said good-bye, it actually felt like he had been sitting in our living room. We were hooked. The next time we connected, he took us on a walking tour of his living quarters including his backyard. Amazing! The word spread as other family members gave Skype a try. It is every grandparent's dream to be able to be face-to-face with a grandchild as they tell you their latest happenings. Gone are all the frustrations that must be endured when there is only a phone connection. One of our little grandchildren had a habit of setting down the phone when she ran off as something caught her eye, leaving us 'talking to the coffee table.'

"Since that first Skype visit, there have been many other online family gatherings. Our little niece and nephew (one-year-old and six-month-old cousins) were visiting together, and we had the great experience of scheduling a 'Skype visit' with them.

The two littlest movie stars were animated and adorable as we tried to engage them. Watching the two interact was just priceless. The six-month-old was anxious to stand up, and this look of absolute incredulity came over the one-year-old's face as he saw his cousin suddenly rising to tower over him. Then, in the next instant, he showed his budding intelligence by staring at her feet, satisfied to see she had 'grown so tall' because she was standing on her mom's knee! Being part of such a precious moment would not have been possible without the bird's-eye view of Skype."

So if you're having a trying day or just need a lift, use the Internet creatively to visit, play, blog, or whatever suits your fancy. An hour or two later, you won't believe how the time has flown.

IF YOU WANT TO FEEL GREAT TODAY . . .

Make the Internet your ally. Thanks to the Internet, the whole world is just a click away. You can learn, see pictures or videos, or speak about almost any subject the world over, with people the world over. Using the Internet, you can visit the Louvre or Iceland or The Sistine Chapel. Be selective, and you can take advantage of the Internet for education or entertainment or research into just about anything of interest or concern. Thanks to services like Skype, you can converse with anyone, anywhere (assuming they have the correct equipment) or arrange an "up close" (video) visit with friends or family far and near, individually or as a group, often for free.

45

Visit the Corn Palace

*The Kennedy Space Center is where they send people to the
    moon,*
The Liberty Bell rang for patriots; a sweet and simple tune.
Mount Rushmore carries faces of presidents, carved out of rock,
*The airplane was made by brothers, in North Carolina's Kitty
    Hawk...*
    – Excerpts from "The ABC Landmarks of the USA"
    by Mr. Flavin's first-grade class

MANY PEOPLE HAVE LIVED IN AN AREA FOR
years and never found their way to some places of
interest right in their own backyard. Landmarks
come in all sizes and shapes and are a great way to remember
the past or celebrate the wonder of God's creation. Every community has a landmark. One of the things Jim and Bobbie love
to do in their travels is to visit as many landmarks as possible.
You cannot help but come away from one of our country's treasured historical landmarks with a renewed sense of patriotism,
marveling at the ingenuity and courage of our forefathers and
feeling more connected to our past. In the same way, a visit to

one of our natural wonders is guaranteed to set your spirit free.

Landmarks in the United States have usually been declared national monuments with the aim of preserving their uniqueness. National monuments must be named by the president. National parks, on the other hand, must also have the approval of Congress. The Antiquities Act of 1906 authorized presidents to name structures of historic or scientific interest and natural geographical sites to be recognized and cared for. The first national monument was Devil's Tower, Wyoming, proclaimed by President Theodore Roosevelt in 1906, followed by the Petrified Forest and the Grand Canyon in Arizona in 1908.

To date, thousands of fascinating landmarks have been declared, two of them by President Bush in 2006. One was the African Burial Ground National Monument, an archaeological site in New York City, and the other the Papahānaumokuākea Marine National Monument in Hawaii, which protects 140,000 square miles of the Pacific Ocean. This marine conservation area is larger than all of America's national parks combined! The northwestern Hawaiian Islands are home to seven thousand marine species, a quarter of which are found nowhere else in the world.

If you love our country as much as we do, you may, like us, be drawn to visit as many of our natural wonders and landmarks as possible. As we (Jim and Bobbie) travel around the country with our work, we usually cannot wait to discover little-known landmarks in our new assignment area. But Bobbie can recall one day when she was a little jet-lagged and more interested in catching her breath with a cup of tea and the newspaper than seeing a landmark on their path to their new city. Jim, on the other hand, tireless explorer that he is, really wanted to stop and see the Corn Palace in Mitchell, South Dakota! Bobbie admits she would rather have done any number of other things than take in this landmark, but she agreed and was so glad she did!

The world's only Corn Palace got its start in 1892 as an exposition where the early settlers displayed the fruits of their harvest to prove it was possible to grow things in South Dakota's soil. These creative pioneers then erected a building whose exterior is completely decorated with elaborate and beautiful murals made of corn, grains, and grasses. The murals are removed and re-created every year using thousands of bushels of raw materials. They provide various glimpses of life in South Dakota and are both unique works of art and a tribute to the agricultural roots of the people. We spent a memorable few hours visiting the Corn Palace as well as the Dakota Discovery Museum and Prehistoric Indian Village. We came away with a renewed appreciation of the culture and artistry of the American Indian tribes as we took a step backward in time with the help of this historical landmark. This introduction gave us a real appreciation for the uniqueness of the Dakotas and set the stage for a wonderful summer among the special people of South Dakota.

Generations of families have made it a priority to visit some of our famous U.S. landmarks. The choices are mind-boggling and sure to inspire even the youngest traveler. A few years ago, *USA Weekend* magazine chose ten landmarks they believed signified defining moments in our country's freedom: Ellis Island in New York; Independence National Historic Park in Philadelphia; the Lincoln Memorial in Washington, D.C.; Jamestown, Virginia; Edmund Pettus Bridge in Selma, Alabama; Esther Morris Statue in Cheyenne, Wyoming; Haymarket Martyr's Statue in Forest Park, Illinois; Saxman Native Village Totem Pole Park in Saxman, Alaska; Kennedy Space Center in Florida; and Walden Pond in Concord, Massachusetts.

Many small, local landmarks exist, and these should never be overlooked. We have often been surprised to discover how many people live in an area but have never visited their own landmark! "Oh, we will do it someday," they assure us. "It's not going anywhere!" Yes, but they are depriving themselves of a transforming few hours. Some of our favorite landmarks are more local than national in nature. For example, we discovered a historical marker on tiny St. Simons Island in Georgia commemorating the significant capture of three British ships during the Revolutionary War, not by power but by ingenuity.

How about setting a goal to see the redwoods in California, majestic Crater Lake in Oregon, the Arch of St. Louis, or the Garden of the Gods in Colorado Springs? Visiting historic churches provides a fascinating glimpse into our country's religious history. Don't pass up an opportunity, for instance, to visit the Church of St. Andrew on Staten Island, New York, founded in 1708. It has quite a story to tell about its 300-year existence and is considered one of the friendliest churches in the valley, still open to God's work and vision.

The next time you are in need of a change of attitude or a new perspective on life, visit a landmark. Go back in time, learn something new, and increase your pride and appreciation for your area or someone else's. Take some advice from Bobbie, who learned an important lesson that day at the Corn Palace. Life is short, and there is so much to see. Don't ever pass up a chance to visit a landmark, even if its name sounds corny!

IF YOU WANT TO FEEL GREAT TODAY . . .

Find a landmark site or location to visit near your home town. Yes, you can see it anytime . . . so why not today? You'll get re-energized about your own region by visiting its landmarks. Let history come alive as you learn about famous local events and people. Or visit our national landmarks, as well.

46

Follow Your Nose

Memories, imagination, old sentiments, and associations are more readily reached through the sense of smell than through any other channel. — *Oliver Wendell Holmes*

SOME SCENTS ARE HEAVENLY AND SOME MAKE us cringe. Yet they share the power to affect our mood and even our overall health. Maybe that's why our nose is in such a prominent place!

It's not hard to imagine Adam and Eve strolling about the Garden of Eden, enjoying the variety of fragrances available to them. We might even think of that as the original aromatherapy. *Well, that was easy enough for them*, you think. *But they weren't bombarded during the day by everything from traffic fumes to soiled diapers . . . well, at least not while they lived in that garden!*

Aromatherapy is defined in the American Council on Science and Health as a "branch" of herbal medicine that centers on using fragrant substances, particularly oily plant extracts, to alter mood or to improve an individual's health.

The alleged benefits of aromatherapy range from stress relief to enhancement of immunity and the unlocking of "emotions from past experiences."[1] These fragrant substances are usually in the form of essential oils that can be massaged into the skin.

Aromatherapy as a concept had its beginning in Europe and Asia in the early 1900s and was used by several French physicians to treat wounds up through World War II. By the 1950s it was gaining more popularity among massage therapist, nurses, and beauticians.

Aromatherapy did not become popular in North America until the 1980s, however, and continues to be controversial among healthcare providers who point out that there are very few evidence-based scientific studies available to prove its usefulness.

Recently some major universities have taken up the challenge and done research studies on aromatherapy, with mixed results. One very large, well-done study at the University of Ohio used two of the most popular aromas, lemon and lavender, but was unable to show improvement in immune status, wound healing, or control of pain. However, lemon did prove to enhance positive moods and help with relaxation among those tested.[2]

While science continues to investigate the merits of aromatherapy, many users of different scents believe that these make them feel relaxed and happier, which in itself is a good thing, even if nothing more than one's mood is "cured."

There have also been recent smaller studies that have found evidence of benefits for the immune system and psychological state. Dr. H. Kuriyama and team found a slight immunologic benefit with aromatherapy and pointed out that their study needed to be validated by a larger patient group.[3] In this study, aromatherapy was combined with massage. The advantage with this treatment is that the scent of the essential oils is inhaled as the oil is absorbed through the skin, thus augmenting the benefits of the massage itself.

Even skeptical subjects may have their opinion changed after their first aromatherapy session. I (Jim) was in the midst of a busy locum tenens assignment in Denver, working long hours and covering several hospitals, when I began to sense stress overload. One day Bobbie and I escaped from the city for a drive in the beautiful Rocky Mountains. We stopped for lunch in Estes Park, and Bobbie noticed a sign for aromatherapy massage. She was sure this would provide a dose of relaxation for her stressed- out husband. I balked at first, believing aromatherapy was not for me! But you can't argue with a nurse for very long and win, so I begrudgingly agreed to try it; it did seem better than touring the local shops. Much to my surprise, I experienced a soothing, relaxing time, permeated by the scent of evergreen and listening to a rushing brook outside the window. I had to admit it did bring my stress quotient way down, and the deep relaxation lasted all day!

Cherie Perez, a research nurse at the world renowned M.D. Anderson Cancer Center, states, "while essential oils may not directly stimulate the immune system, they can complement cancer treatment by boosting the system's ability to fight off infection. Since it has many potential uses ranging from managing anxiety and nausea to helping with sleep, general relaxation, memory, and attention, many individuals, including cancer patients, can benefit from aromatherapy."[4]

Perez recommends these five oils in particular:

1. Lavender to treat insomnia, migraines, and provide stress relief; 2. Rosemary to relieve muscle pain, low blood pressure, and to help with cold feet and hands; 3. Spearmint to aid digestion and ease nausea and vomiting; 4. Bay Laurel; and, 5. Ylang Ylang— these last two appealing to men to and treat skin rashes, rheumatism, and stomach ailments.

Other studies suggest, ". . . that when essential oils (particularly rose, lavender, and frankincense) were used by qualified midwives, pregnant women felt less anxiety and fear, had a stronger sense of well-being, and had less need for pain medications during delivery. Many women also report that peppermint oil relieves nausea and vomiting during labor."[5]

Does aromatherapy sound like something you would like to try out to perk up your day and enhance your health? We recommend making an appointment with a certified aroma therapist because they will be able not only to direct you to the ideal scents for you personally but also will help you avoid any of the negative effects that can occur if you are a novice.

Practitioners warn of dangerous side effects such as burns, respiratory problems, or even negative interactions with medication you may be taking. Be advised that the commercial products that surround us are often synthetic fragrances and very few contain the essential oils. Some of these products are not recommended by professionals due to problems with impurities. For instance, some candles and incense produce a soot that can irritate the lungs. To locate an aromatherapist near you, contact the National Association of Holistic Therapy at www.naha.org.

With the guidance of a knowledgeable practitioner, you can try different scents to see how they affect you and your family.

IF YOU WANT TO FEEL GREAT TODAY . . .

Spice up your day with healthy and mood enhancing aromas. Boost your relaxation and happiness quotient with aromatherapy. You can start simply with things like scented candles, room sprays, air fresheners, or potpourri. But we also recommend you consult a qualified aromatherapist to get you started on a path toward improved stress relief using this method.

········· **47** ···········

Keep Company With "My Left Foot"

I complained that I had no shoes, till I met a man who had no feet.
— Anonymous

JENNY'S FIVE-YEAR-OLD BECAME ILL AND ALMOST died of an undiagnosed illness. Over the first few months of what would become years, the child became totally disabled and dependent before slowly starting to improve. Life became one long string of visits to doctors, physical therapists, special-education teachers, and counselors, and in the midst of it all, Jenny had to learn how best to advocate for her child's special needs. It was nearly all she could do, day by day, to keep the schedule straight and her child comfortable. "Put On a Happy Face" was definitely not her theme song, and exhaustion became her constant companion. Yet she did maintain a cheerful demeanor through it all and remained strong for her child, who eventually recovered most of her abilities and graduated from college. The story could have been made into a movie. Maybe it will be.

Stories about overcoming adversity or achieving the seemingly impossible against overwhelming odds inspire us. And when we hear about them, see them in movie form, read about them in a book, see them depicted in a play, or even hear them described in music, we're reminded that our situation, as difficult as it may seem to be, may actually be manageable if we can learn from those who have walked the path before us and found at least one way to survive or even to thrive.

One of my (Dave's) favorite ways to bolster my sense of hope when I feel down is to watch inspirational movies. Sometimes this means watching a movie with a spiritual or biblical or even specifically Christian message. Your list will undoubtedly differ from mine, and some listed are not specifically "Christian," yet still worth watching. I have appreciated such movies (or movie series) as: *The Chronicles of Narnia, The Lord of the Rings, Facing the Giants, The Ten Commandments, Ben Hur, The Passion of the Christ, Chariots of Fire, The Sound of Music, Something the Lord Made* and *The Mission.* And I'm told that I should see *The End of the Spear, Fireproof, Joseph, Jacob, Matthew, Hachi, The Ultimate Gift, The Blind Side, Christy, Because of Winn-Dixie, Anne of Green Gables, Heidi,* and *Gifted Hands,* among others.

Of course, many movies without specifically Christian content are also considered inspirational. Online you can find several lists—one is the American Film Institute's (AFI) list of "100 Most Inspiring Films of All Time"[1] and the other is MovieFone's (MF) list of the twenty-five "Most Inspirational Movies of All Time."[2] Since I either own or have viewed about forty films from the top 100 list, there's a lot of inspiration still out there for me.

Here are the top twenty-five of the AFI's list of 100, based on choices submitted by 1,500 film artists, critics, and historians from a ballot of over 300 nominated films. MovieFone's rankings of the same films are noted, as appropriate, after AFI's ranking:

1. *It's a Wonderful Life* (1946)—#4 on the MF list
2. *To Kill a Mockingbird* (1962)
3. *Schindler's List* (1993)—#6 on MF's list
4. *Rocky* (1976)—#5 on MF's list
5. *Mr. Smith Goes to Washington* (1939)—#21 on MF's list
6. *E.T.: The Extra-Terrestrial* (1982)
7. *The Grapes of Wrath* (1940)—#10 on MF's list
8. *Breaking Away* (1979)
9. *Miracle on 34th Street* (1947)
10. *Saving Private Ryan* (1998)
11. *The Best Years of Our Lives* (1946)—#7 on MF's list
12. *Apollo 13* (1995)
13. *Hoosiers* (1986)—#9 on MF's list
14. *The Bridge on the River Kwai* (1957)—#11 on MF's list
15. *The Miracle Worker* (1962)—#3 on MF's list
16. *Norma Rae* (1979)—#8 on MF's list
17. *One Flew Over the Cuckoo's Nest* (1975)
18. *The Diary of Anne Frank* (1959)—#19 on MF's list
19. *The Right Stuff* (1983)
20. *Philadelphia* (1993)—#16 on MF's list
21. *In the Heat of the Night* (1967)—#23 on MF's list
22. *The Pride of the Yankees* (1942)
23. *The Shawshank Redemption* (1994)—#18 on MF's list
24. *National Velvet* (1944)
25. *Sullivan's Travels* (1941)

The others from the MovieFone list are:

#1 *My Left Foot* (1989)
#2 *Glory* (1989)
#12 *Remember the Titans* (2000)
#13 *Hotel Rwanda* (2004)
#14 *Erin Brockovich* (2000)

#15 *Field of Dreams* (1989)
#17 *A Raisin in the Sun* (1961)
#20 *Chariots of Fire* (1981)
#22 *Rudy* (1994)
#24 *Stand and Deliver* (1988)
#25 *Forrest Gump* (1994)

So what am I going to do? I am going to watch *My Left Foot* as soon as I can. It's the true story of Christy Brown, an Irishman born with cerebral palsy. Paralyzed from birth, he was written off as retarded and helpless. But his mother never gave up on him. He learned to write using his left foot. He became a well-known author, painter, and fundraiser, despite his multiple challenges. This film was nominated for the Academy Awards for Best Picture, Best Director, and Best Adapted Screenplay. One actor and one actress won Academy Awards for their performances. Having looked disability in the eye, I consider this film one I must see, even if it didn't make AFI's list at all.

IF YOU WANT TO FEEL GREAT TODAY . . .

Let an inspirational movie move and motivate you. The combination of sight, sound, music, acting, and story imbeds the images and experience deep within. You can change your mood and perspective quickly by watching a good movie. Movies can be good "therapy," able to affect your outlook and inspire you to attempt greater things. Look over our list of movies, add you own, and invite friends or family over to watch one or more . . . don't forget the popcorn!

48

Unfold Your Family Life

I have been the faithful photographer of the family for thirty years. Scrapbooking was a great way to bring my many photos to life.
— Anonymous

WHEN WE WERE YOUNG, SOME PEOPLE (usually girls) kept diaries. Many of their entries started with "Dear Diary," and they poured out their heart day by day, sometimes including a photograph or other printed clipping to accompany that day's entry. Now many of these same women are part of a movement called "scrapbooking." Using modern methods, materials, and technology—including scanners and the Internet, where one can produce a digital "scrapbook" online—millions are creating family heirlooms using photographs (old and new) with accompanying narrative.

This type of history-keeping can be traced back to ancient Greece. In the seventeenth century, Francis Bacon and John Milton created "commonplace books," precursors of modern scrapbooking. Later Thomas Jefferson and Mark Twain also kept notes and various memorabilia that might be considered "scrapbooking" today—without the photos, of course, since modern photography on the lay level only became available at the beginning of the twentieth century.

The development of modern scrapbooking is often attributed to Marielen Christensen of Spanish Fork, Utah. According to Wikipedia, Christensen "began designing creative pages for her family's photo memories, inserting the completed pages into sheet protectors collected in 3-ring binders. By 1980, she had assembled over fifty volumes and was invited to display them at the World Conference on Records in Salt Lake City. Marielen and her husband A. J. authored and published a how-to book, *Keeping Memories Alive*, and opened a scrapbook store in 1981 that remains open today."[1]

One of our scrapbooking friends (sometimes called "scrappers") said, "Scrapbooking can be rather complicated and overwhelming unless done in little steps or little books. It can be a long-term commitment to take an event or period of time and photographically, biographically, and artfully construct something very meaningful with a written story to go with it. It is like writing a book. But even young moms can do it in little bits.

"As I approached having an empty nest," our friend wrote, "I knew that I could sit around and watch TV all the time, or I could develop a few hobbies that I could be passionate about instead. One was genealogy, and the other was scrapbooking. Scrapbooking has been around forever, but the latest trends have made it a craze for good reason. It takes the simple concept of a photo album and makes it a more purposeful book. As I saw the potential of this craft by going to scrapbooking parties, reading scrapbooking magazines, and watching women create masterpieces at our scrapbooking retreats, I took up scrapbooking and have encouraged every woman in my season of life to join me."

The creation of a new scrapbook is like watching your family life unfold all over again, with pictures of your children as babies, then as little boys and girls, and, finally, as adults. It helps you feel fulfillment as a parent to know that you have left a legacy in photos and words for each of your children's homes and families. The photos may make you laugh at how silly everybody looked thirty years ago! And sometimes they make you pause and think of someone—a family member or pet—who has passed away. Scrapbooking is a great way to lift your spirits even as you weep over joyful sentimental memories!

Scrapbook companies are developing little story-size scrapbooks in the form of ready-to-finish small accordion books, desktop photo scrapbook cubes, and even some as small as a luggage tag, according to our friend. Some projects can be done in a few hours, and some take quite a lot longer. Many women spend up to a year just making one album. Others who are looking for fast and easy projects can find ready-made background papers. Some albums have been developed so that all you need to do is slip photos in and add embellishments and a quick caption to each picture. The only limit is your creativity.

"Now that the girls are out of the house," our friend added, "I am still working on their life stories by scrapbooking, but now the magic of technology has enabled me to take the really not-so-good photos of thirty years ago, improve them, crop them, digitalize them, and make many copies of them. Once the photos are scanned in and digitalized, I can, in quiet moments with my laptop, create an amazing scrapbook without all the paper, glue, scissors, and other endless supplies—even the physical photos! Or I can just upload my photos from my camera to any number of digital scrapbooking services online, add templates and journaling to my photos, and end up with a really nice scrapbook that can be copied as many times as I want, sent via e-mail, or physically published into a high-quality book or books."

Scrapbooking can have very healthy sociological or even spiritual value too, as many "scrappers" get together locally or in larger groups at retreats or in similar settings. Our friend, who organizes some of these retreats, recently wrote to her "scrappers" about her daughter Jessica's outdoor wedding, which was interrupted by a downpour. "Memories are important to our souls. That's why our bi-annual 'Memories That Matter' retreats have been so popular. Scrapbooking, complete with journaling of everyday events, is an incredibly important call on our lives. As women, we can be scribes of the silly, happy, spiritual, and even sad moments of our lives, complete with instant emotion every time we remember. This is deep soul stuff. I will never forget how gingerly five people lifted Jessica's gorgeous $800 dress past the mud and accompanied her through that moment in her life. I can't wait to do the scrapbook with that story and picture."[2]

IF YOU WANT TO FEEL GREAT TODAY . . .

Become a scrapper. Start that book about your family that you've always wanted to create. Combine your journals with photos of family events and you'll have your masterpiece. With modern digital technology you can breathe new life into old photos and add them to your life story in ways that were unimagined in our youth. That being so, and the digital revolution being what it is, just imagine what will be possible in just a few more years—3D, talking scrapbooks with digital video complete with input for all the senses? Probably more than that, but for now you can establish a family history library that others will draw upon later. Maybe someone will even do a scrapbook of you doing your scrapbook!

.... **49** ....

Relish Some Relics

Museums and art stores are also sources of pleasure and in-
spiration. . . . I derive genuine pleasure from touching great
works of art. As my fingertips trace line and curve, they dis-
cover the thought and emotion which the artist has portrayed.
                                                    – Helen Keller

HAS IT EVER BEEN YOUR EXPERIENCE THAT
company often comes knocking in the middle of a
downpour, a snowstorm, or on the hottest day of the
year? You have been looking forward to a great visit, but sitting
around the house all day attempting some adult conversation
and keeping the kids from becoming bored could turn the day
into an endurance contest. One great way to create a wonderful
memory is to visit a museum together.

Some of us can remember walking through dusty rooms full
of old relics, dead butterflies, and scary masks. We were under
the watchful eye of the museum guard to be sure we didn't talk
too loud or touch anything! By comparison, today's museums
are a breath of fresh air, masterpieces of learning and involvement. Visitors are encouraged to interact with the displays, and

all ages come away energized and enlightened. There are thousands of amazing choices, and, depending on where you live, you can choose from a variety of different themes. There are art museums, science museums, music museums, cultural museums, history museums, and even museums that depict highlights of a city. In Vermont you can visit the Maple Sugar Museum. In Wisconsin you can visit the Spinning Top and Yo-Yo Museum. Or how about painting your own pottery in Portland or "petting" the ocean creatures on the Jersey Shore? Every region across our country has something unique to celebrate, and usually there is a museum where we can learn details we would otherwise miss.

Learning takes place through several avenues. Some of us are visual learners, others are auditory learners, and still others learn by doing. Now that scientists have discovered more about the process of learning, museums are designing exhibits to facilitate everyone's style. This almost always captures the interest of children as well as adults.

The Chicago History Museum, for instance, will convince any visitor that history is a fascinating subject! If you visit www.chicagohistory.org/kidsfamilies/plan visit/index, you will discover the unique learning stations waiting for you there. Adults and kids can create their own bridge, ride a high-wheel bike down a wood-paved street, hear the Great Chicago Fire, catch a fly ball at the ball park, smell their way around town using the Smell Map, become a Chicago hot dog, or create their own giant-sized postcard of their visit! Sounds like a lot of fun, doesn't it?

We (Jim and Bobbie) have been privileged to visit many different museums as we travel with our work or visit with family. One memorable afternoon we visited a science museum with our kids and our three granddaughters. Their ages at that time were one, four, and six years old. Quite a diverse, lively group! It was a fabulous museum full of a whole range of exciting exhibits and opportunities. As we walked through the door, we barely had time to get our hand stamped before visual overload took control. Our one-year-old made a beeline for the colorful light displays, which kept her attention longer than any one activity had previously done. The four-year-old was fascinated by the wind tunnel and wave display and wanted to experience all the sensations offered by this great interactive tool. She was just having fun, but a whole lot of learning was going on! Meanwhile our six-year-old was fascinated by the "TV station" where kids could actually practice broadcasting the weather.

Another big hit with all of us was the health center where kids could pump blood through a circulatory system or rotate bones into different positions to learn what happens when we run or throw a ball. We adults also had a chance to learn why turning doorknobs or bending certain ways is getting more challenging! How thankful we were that we had four adults available to follow the kids' interests, and we loved being able to become kids ourselves for an afternoon.

Another time we spent a fun few hours in St. Louis visiting the Gateway Arch and museum. The museum depicted the genius of the engineering feat necessary to build the gigantic arch on the banks of the mighty Mississippi River. A movie not only traced the building process but also celebrated the drama of opening up the river as a way to transport people and goods by water back in the nineteenth century. It also serves as a memorial to the contribution Thomas Jefferson made to westward expansion by making possible Lewis and Clark's remarkable journey. It was good fodder for an animated discussion with our granddaughter about these early heroes.

Then we were able to board the unique elevator-like pod to ride 630 feet to the top of the arch. What a thrill! From this vantage point we could see for miles in every direction and watch the constant parade of boats on the river.

One snowy, blustery day while visiting our daughter, we took our young granddaughter to the Smithsonian. What an invigorating place this is. The first step is to choose which building you will concentrate on, or you could be there all through the night! Our granddaughter loves animals, so we chose the Natural History Museum. It was fun to help her identify the different animals and how they live. The monstrous dinosaur was a real hit; we had a lively discussion about how dinosaurs lived and where they went!

Visiting a museum is sure to transform your day, teach you something new, and make memories. It can be a solitary experience where you spend a few relaxing hours wandering through an art museum, or it can be a high-energy activity where a family plays and learns together. Either way, be on the lookout for museums to visit in your hometown and as you have opportunities to visit different areas of our country. You will be glad you did.

IF YOU WANT TO FEEL GREAT TODAY . . .

Relive history by visiting a museum, where history's tastes, sounds, looks, and feel are preserved. In today's museums, you are not just viewing it or hearing about it. You're being there. If you want to transform an ordinary day into a high-powered learning experience, step into a museum. Explore your area's museums and those in your path as you travel. You will create great memories, broaden your knowledge, and have a lot of fun.

50

Take up the True First Occupation

Gardening is about enjoying the smell of things growing in the soil, getting dirty without feeling guilty, and generally taking the time to soak up a little peace and serenity.
– Lindley Karstens

MENTION YARD WORK OR GARDENING TO some people and they cringe at the thought of spending their weekends mowing, raking, trimming, and pulling weeds. In fact, many hire someone to do it just to free up their time. Mention yard work to others and they smile in delight at the opportunity to spend time outdoors communing with nature. In fact, they can't wait to get through the dormant winter to when things can be planted in spring and in full bloom during the summer.

For sure, yard work can get old when it has to be done week after week. However, in recent years, gardening has taken on renewed popularity as people have gotten more health conscious and have begun tightening their belts in a shrinking economy.

During tough economic times, more and more people are doing their own yard work as well as planting vegetable gardens to feed their families. Seed companies report increased sales during hard financial times. "Interest in growing fruits and vegetables picks up during economic downturns. Seed companies say that a dime spent on seeds yields about $1.00 worth of produce. Bad economic times can also mean more time to garden—people who cancel their summer vacations are around to water their tomatoes."[1]

Vegetable gardening is gaining in popularity because it is consistent with what might be described as a "prudent way of life"—an approach to providing food and other necessities for one's family as independently as possible versus presuming that access to these necessities will be available whenever they are needed. From homesteaders to homemakers, many people are growing produce to feed their families with fresh vegetables during harvest time, while also filling their pantries with preserved nutritious whole foods where the climate does not allow for outdoor growing year round.

Gardening has a long history, beginning of course with the biblical Garden of Eden. Lush and green, it supplied all that was needed to sustain life. Our forefathers lived off the land when gardening was a necessity and a way of life. Many of us remember the gardens our grandparents tended and especially the fresh fare at mealtimes.

During World War II, food was rationed and people were encouraged to grow "Victory Gardens" to show their support for the war effort. In the ensuing years of economic growth, when food was plentiful and could be purchased from the grocery store, gardening became a hobby instead of a means of survival.

Don't have a green thumb? Thankfully, a green thumb is something that can be developed with time, ingenuity, and a small financial investment. Start small by staking out a place in your yard that you want to designate for a garden. Visit your local garden center and talk with a salesperson about the equipment you might need. The bare necessities, such as a hose, rake, hoe, shovel, and various hand tools, can be purchased at a low cost. If you're not sure about your soil, take a small sample with you and ask what you will need for optimum soil preparation and what will grow the best with what you have to work with. You can purchase plants that are ready to put in the soil, or you can start from seeds.

If you are going to grow vegetables, start with something easy for the beginning gardener. Tomatoes are always a good bet and are easy to grow. Peppers, salad greens, and squash are also good choices. Strawberries grow well in the ground and in containers.

Container gardening is growing in popularity, especially for those who have limited space. Containers are easy and affordable and work well in many different spaces. And for a variety of color, containers are ideal. Almost any vegetable or plant can be grown in a container. Container gardens are also good for the environment as they give off oxygen and eat up carbon dioxide. No room outside? Containers are ideal for inside your home or on a patio or deck.

A relatively new concept is called aeroponic gardening, in which high tech methods are used to grow flowers or vegetables from holes in a plastic tower that holds whatever plants you wish to grow, with the plants being sustained by nutrients delivered directly to their roots via water that is pumped from below. No soil is used. If you've ever visited the hydroponic gardens at EPCOT center in Orlando, Florida, you are familiar with this concept.

If you don't choose to grow vegetables, flowers and other plants are also fun to grow and tend. In the spring your local garden center has a plethora of annuals and other plants to choose from. Decide what you like, what will grow best in your garden conditions (type of soil, sun, shade, climate, etc.) and what is easiest for you to care for, and prepare to enjoy a "riot of color." Bulbs can be planted in the fall, providing beautiful color and variety in the spring. Garden magazines galore and plenty of information on the Internet will give you ideas on how to be creative with what you have to work with.

In addition to the obvious health benefits from growing your own vegetables, there are other benefits to tending your garden. Some of the physical benefits include fresh air and exercise. It's a good way to burn calories. As someone said, "Gardening is a labor of love. A treadmill is just labor."

As you improve your strength and endurance, you are also helping to prevent such chronic conditions as obesity, high blood pressure, and osteoporosis. It's also a great brain workout in that it requires creativity and planning.

Psychological benefits abound. The satisfaction gained from spending time in your garden and watching your plants grow goes a long way toward relieving stress. Just the fact that this is your achievement, your success, gets you involved in something bigger than yourself and can play an important role in helping you to be emotionally healthier.[2]

Gardening can also provide a social outlet as you connect and share with others about your mutual gardening experiences. Many communities have garden clubs. In the spring, garden tours are common, giving you the opportunity to "harvest" growing ideas from others. Gardening is a great way to get your children or grandchildren involved. Give them a plot of land or part of your garden that is their responsibility to cultivate, and share their excitement as the plants grow.

Many people also report the opportunity to slow down and commune with their Creator while tending his creation. Gardening was, after all, the real first occupation.[3]

"I've never had a green thumb," said Jan. "But I love the out-

212 ✦ 52 WAYS TO FEEL GREAT TODAY

doors and thought it might be fun to try my hand at gardening. I have a small space and knew that I'd have to start small. I went to my local garden center and found them to be very helpful. I came away with some tomato plants and several varieties of flowers. Some I put in the ground and others I put in containers spaced colorfully around my porch and patio. Imagine my excitement when they all did well. I enjoyed those tomatoes for months. Perhaps the best advice I got, however, was, 'When weeding, the best way to make sure you are removing a weed and not a valuable plant is to pull on it. If it comes out of the ground easily, it is a valuable plant.'"

So grab those tools and get set for a renewing adventure in your own backyard.

IF YOU WANT TO FEEL GREAT TODAY . . .

Remember that nature is God's classroom. Grow something from his earth and you will find yourself growing with God. Relish the fact that gardening harnesses your attention and "plants" you close to the earth. Engage your body, your senses, your brain, and your spirit as you create your personal beautiful, and sometimes edible, living space. Enjoy the fruits of your labor as your flowers or vegetables are harvested and shared.

51

Just Breathe . . . Correctly

*Practicing regular, mindful breathing can be calming and en-
ergizing and can even help with stress-related health problems
ranging from panic attacks to digestive disorders.*
                                                    – Andrew Weil, MD

MOST OF US ARE WELL AWARE THAT WE
should eat right, exercise regularly, get plenty of rest,
and lead otherwise balanced lives in order to maintain optimum health. But, did you know that something you do
without even thinking about it—some 20,000 times a day—is
equally as important in maintaining your health?

Breathing keeps us alive and serves two basic functions: It
helps transport oxygen to various parts of the body, and it helps
to eliminate waste products (carbon dioxide) through the lymphatic system. The more oxygen we take in through breathing
correctly, the more efficiently our circulatory and lymphatic systems work. Improper functioning of these metabolic systems
can lead to health-related issues over time.

Watch a baby breathing, and you'll notice that they take deep
breaths from their bellies, moving their diaphragms up and

down. As we age, however, and our lives get busier and more complicated, we exchange healthy deep breathing for shallow chest breathing. Standing up straight, sucking in our guts, and puffing out our chests may look great, but it isn't the best for our health. As shallow chest breathers, we are only using the middle and upper portions of our lungs, which limits optimum oxygen consumption.

According to Marcell Pick, "The best oxygen exchange comes from breathing deep around the naval instead of the upper chest. You should think about filling up your belly when you take a deep breath."[1]

To find out if you are a shallow breather, put your hand on your abdomen and breathe through your nose. If your chest puffs out and your abdomen deflates, you are a shallow breather. To correct this, inhale deeply and slowly through your nose into your abdomen. You should feel your abdomen rise and your chest should move just a little. Exhale through your mouth.

Practice this three or four times until you are doing it correctly. You may want to practice while sitting in a comfortable chair in case you feel dizzy or lightheaded from over-oxygenation. It is important to learn to breathe correctly, but be careful to let your body get used to all that extra oxygen.

As you practice these and other breathing exercises a few times each day, you should soon be learning to breathe correctly all the time, which should help you reach a more relaxed state consistently. You can call on your specific deep breathing exercises during times of stress, anxiety, insomnia, and at other moments when life becomes chaotic.

"As a therapist, my life is very stressful at times, especially when I don't take time for myself," said Sue. "When this happens, I've noticed my anxiety level increasing, I have more aches and pains, and have more difficulty sleeping. To help relieve the stress and anxiety, I've learned to stop during the day and take a few minutes just to breathe deeply and to clear and focus my mind."

Additional benefits of deep breathing:

Aids Relaxation: "Slow, deep breathing is a powerful anti-stress technique. When you bring air down into the lower portion of the lungs, where the oxygen exchange is more efficient, heart rate slows, blood pressure decreases, muscles relax, anxiety eases, and the mind calms."[2]

Reduces Hot Flashes: Studies have linked focused breathing with reducing hot flashes in menopausal women, relieving chronic pain, and reducing symptoms of PMS.[3]

Counters Mood Disorders: "Richard Brown, MD, and Patricia Gerbard, MD, reported that deep-breathing techniques were extremely effective in handling depression, anxiety, and stress related disorders."[4]

Enhances Exercise Benefits: "Deep breathing delivers many of the benefits of exercise, including facilitating weight loss. Though not a substitute for exercise, it's a great first step for those just beginning an exercise plan, and deep breathing enhances the benefits of any form of exercise."[5]

Opens Airways: "For several years, researchers have known that deep breaths benefit the lungs of healthy individuals by pushing open narrowed airways. Researchers at Johns Hopkins University have discovered

. . . .

that deep breaths also provide protection by preventing airways from closing in the first place—a real boon to asthma sufferers and others who suffer with breathing related illnesses."[6]

Deep breathing can increase your productivity, too, by counteracting stress and increasing your energy. "Learning techniques of deep breathing has helped me live more or less constantly with the stress of deadlines," says William C., a publisher. "And I believe it has even increased my enjoyment of doing something I love, even when I have to stay very focused on my work for long periods of time. Even after just a few deep breathing exercises in the morning, it's hard to believe how much more energized I feel."

IF YOU WANT TO FEEL GREAT TODAY . . .

Just breathe . . . correctly. This is extremely important, not only to your health but to your quality of life. Stress relief, improved digestion, and lung function are just a few of the many important benefits. Since breathing correctly does not "come naturally" except for babies, do yourself a big favor—learn and practice deep breathing and then breathe in a richer, fuller life.

52

Expect Rain

*Never let go of hope. One day you will see that it all has fi-
nally come together. . . . You will look back and laugh at what
has passed and you will ask yourself . . . "How did I get
through all of that?"*   *– Jancari Campi*

AS HENRY WADSWORTH LONGFELLOW WROTE,
"Into each life some rain must fall." Most of us have
days, weeks, or even longer periods of time in which
we feel down, discouraged, troubled, or perhaps even a touch
of despair. When these feelings come, you can work your way
through if you allow the things you know to control the things
you feel.

Earlier in the same poem quoted above, Longfellow also
wrote, "Be still, sad heart, and cease repining; Behind the clouds
is the sun still shining." In the sometimes harsh environment
(Colorado, elevation 8,200 to 10,000 feet) where I (Dave) have
spent most of my time for the past few years, it can be difficult
to remember when the snow is flying and the wind is howling
that above those storm clouds, the sun really is still shining.

By experience we know that if we wait long enough, the storm will pass and the sun will come out again, even if it takes five days as it did a couple winters ago when a single late-winter storm dumped over seventy inches of snow on the home we owned there.

The storms of life come in many forms, including illness, financial hardship, relational difficulties, accidents, legal issues, problems with one's kids, loss of a loved one, or even loss of a beloved pet. Sometimes there's a crisis. Sometimes the problems are more long-term. Having been there and done both, the first thing I'd like you to know if you're feeling down is that pain is pain. It doesn't matter so much what the source of it is; every person journeys through his or her own "lonesome valley" uniquely, and the point is not how they make it but that they *do eventually make it through.*

Since no one else can understand or know exactly how you feel, you have our permission to ignore those who afflict you with various irrelevant and ignorant pieces of advice or even criticize you for feeling what you feel in light of whatever circumstances you are struggling with, as if such words could "cheer you up."

Yes, you might be able to find someone who has it worse than you do or better than you do. But you simply cannot find anyone who has it exactly the way you do, in the present moment, when you're looking despair in the eye. Hope is what you need, not pious platitudes, for hope is, as the New Testament says, "an anchor for the soul" (Hebrews 6:19).

As I write this, it has been more than thirty years since my first son died. In those three decades I've experienced and written about times of deep struggle, depression, and near hopelessness, including that very dark time a few years after Jonathan died when my second son, Chris, got sick and almost died of the same illness that had taken his brother.

Hope was what kept me alive, inside and out, and kept me

moving forward even when the temptation to give up was strong. I wrote this poem in the midst of such a time:

> I look into the Father's eyes
> And wrestle with a thousand "Whys"
> Why this? Why now? Why him, not I?
> Why us, not them? I can't disguise
> The hurt, the rage, unbridled pain
> Erupting from my soul, again.
> If that's the way it's going to be
> Then build Your Kingdom without me.
>
> But then, again, where could I go
> To hear a word of hope, and know
> The promise that beyond the pain
> The ballad has a glad refrain?
> But what for now? And how can one
> Still vocalize "Thy will be done"?
>
> And soon I hear a song begin,
> Celestial, but from deep within,
> A new, yet ancient melody
> Of joy and pain, disharmony.
> Or do the strains combine somehow,
> A lovely paradox of sound?[1]

Hope is the antidote for discouragement or despair. But the long-term effect of this antidote is totally dependent on the trustworthiness of the person we are trusting to take us through our discouragement or despair to something other. No human person is worthy of this trust. No philosophy or religious perspective is worthy, either. In my own experience, only One is worthy—the One who always keeps his promises.

IF YOU WANT TO FEEL HOPE TODAY . . .

• List the things you are hoping for right now. Cross out any that are expectations instead of hopes. Next to the ones that represent true hopes, write the reason for your hope.

• Write down different aspects of mental health that you believe hope may affect. Ask yourself: If I could increase my hope, could that turn a stormy day into a sunny one?

• Ask yourself if it is hard for you to have hope because you can't control the outcome of something that is troubling you. If so, how might you counter this?

• Try to picture hope. What images come to mind? If you are artistic, sketch or draw a picture, or find one that expresses hope. If you have difficulty with renewing your sense of hope, post that picture where you will see it on a regular basis.

• Reflect on the biblical passage about hope being an anchor for the soul, meditating on the meaning and importance of that statement. Keep a record of your insights, and return to them when you experience a "storm" in your life.

• Find other trustworthy sayings, and keep them in a place where you can review them when you need an ounce of hope to counter a pound of despair. The Old Testament psalmists often struggled with discouragement. In Psalm 42:11 the psalmist described how his own hope was renewed: "Why are you downcast, O my soul, Why so disturbed within me? Put your hope in God; for I will yet praise him, my Savior and my God."

About The Authors

Dr. David B. Biebel is a minister, author, and editor. He holds the Doctor of Ministry degree in Personal Wholeness from Gordon-Conwell Theological Seminary. He edited the Christian Medical & Dental Associations' flagship journal *Today's Christian Doctor* from 1992 to 2011, before joining the staff of Florida Hospital's Publishing division as Managing Editor. Dr. Biebel has authored or co-authored nineteen books, including three with the Dills. His hobbies include hunting, fishing, camping, golf, mushrooming, and cooking for his wife, Ilona, and their English Springer Spaniel, Baxter. They live in Florida.

James E. Dill, MD, is a board-certified gastroenterologist with over forty years of practice experience. He is a locum tenens physician and is at present practicing in Hawaii. He is the co-author of three books including this one, *Your Mind at Its Best*, and *The A to Z Guide to Healthier Living.* His special interests include photography and paddleboarding.

Bobbie Dill, RN, has served as a nurse in various specialties, including gastroenterology nursing, psychiatric nursing, camp nursing, ER, med-legal consulting and school nursing, and is the co-author (with her husband, Jim) of nineteen journal articles and three books, including this one. She and her husband were among the first husband-wife Christian medical teams to help establish a truly wholistic medical practice in the U.S. While serving in Hawaii, they enjoy their periodic medical work at a hospital in American Samoa, and are trying their best to learn the Samoan and Hawaiian languages. Her hobbies include racewalking with Jim.

The authors' goal is to help people attain and maintain optimal health so they can love the Lord with their whole heart, soul, mind, and strength, and their neighbors as themselves.

Appendix:
The Healthy 100 Connection

I MAGINE A BODY THAT IS HEALTHY AND STRONG, A spirit that is vibrant and refreshed, and a life that glorifies God. Can you imagine living to a Healthy 100? Why not join the movement? The Healthy 100 movement unites the best of science and the best of faith with the goal of equipping people to live long, vibrant lives filled with power, passion, and purpose.

The invitation to imagine a Healthy 100 is not a warranty or guarantee—it's an opportunity. An opportunity to examine the best practices of the longest living people in the world and learn their secrets.

What are these longevity secrets? They are contained in the CREATION Health acronym. CREATION Health is a remarkable plan for healthy living based on eight original principles found in the creation story in the book of Genesis. Rightly applied, these principles can help you achieve mental, physical, spiritual and emotional well being. Each letter of the word CREATION stands for one of the eight principles. C – Choice, R – Rest, E – Environment, A – Activity, T – Trust, I – Interpersonal, O – Outlook, N – Nutrition. These eight essentials meld together to form the blueprint for health we yearn for and the life we are intended to live.

If you would like to discover more about the Healthy 100 movement and the CREATION Health lifestyle, there are many resources available including books, music, videos, websites, seminars, and events. See the "Resources" section at the end of this book to learn more.

The ideas presented in *52 Ways to Feel Great Today* serve as a perfect complement to the principles of CREATION Health and the Healthy 100 movement. In this Appendix you will find a complete list of the chapters in this book along with a reference to which of the eight principles the chapter relates too. Why not encourage your business, church, or small group to read this book and the CREATION Health books together. Join the Healthy 100 movement and set up a seminar that can benefit your whole community. The possibilities are great!

Connection to CREATION Health Principles

1. Turn Pretzels Into Thanksgiving Dinners
   Principles: *Interpersonal, Outlook, Nutrition*
2. Make a Love Alphabet—For Yourself
   Principles: *Choice, Trust, Outlook*
3. Go Brain Jogging
   Principles: *Choice, Activity, Outlook*
4. Count Something Other Than Beans
   Principles: *Interpersonal, Outlook*
5. Cook Up Love in the Kitchen
   Principles: *Choice, Interpersonal, Nutrition*
6. Color Your World
   Principles: *Choice, Environment, Outlook*
7. Get Out of That Rut!
   Principles: *Outlook*
8. Rent a Puppy, Kitten, or Kid
   Principles: *Interpersonal, Outlook*
9. See God's Glory in Every Place
   Principles: *Choice, Trust, Outlook*
10. Discover Your Mode of Expression
    Principles: *Environment, Outlook*
11. Catch the Experience
    Principles: *Rest, Environment, Interpersonal*
12. Try Airborne Ecotherapy
    Principles: *Environment, Activity, Outlook*
13. Loins Cloths and Clubs Not Required
    Principles: *Choice, Activity, Outlook*
14. Get Wet
    Principles: *Environment, Activity, Interpersonal*
15. Better Than an Antidepressant
    Principles: *Choice, Activity, Interpersonal*
16. Delight in the Elements
    Principles: *Environment, Trust, Outlook*

35. Go Where the Wild Things Are
    Principles: *Environment, Interpersonal*
36. Become Not Like the Tin Man
    Principles: *Activity, Outlook*
37. Stop Fixin' to do Something
    Principles: *Choice, Outlook, Environment*
38. Unearth Those Skeletons
    Principles: *Interpersonal, Outlook*
39. Rock On, Groove to the Beat, or Hum with a Hymn
    Principles: *Environment, Choice, Outlook*
40. Hang Ten!
    Principles: *Choice, Activity*
41. Try a "Spice to Life" Meal
    Principles: *Nutrition, Outlook, Choice*
42. Tune to the Maker's Channel
    Principles: *Environment, Trust, Outlook*
43. Set Sail for New Adventures
    Principles: *Outlook*
44. Go Surfing With No Board
    Principles: *Outlook, Interpersonal*
45. Visit the Corn Palace
    Principles: *Activity, Outlook*
46. Follow Your Nose
    Principles: *Environment, Outlook*
47. Keep Company With "My Left Foot"
    Principles: *Outlook*
48. Unfold Your Family Life
    Principles: *Choice, Interpersonal*
49. Relish Some Relics
    Principles: *Activity, Outlook*
50. Take Up the True First Occupation
    Principles: *Environment, Activity, Nutrition*
51. Just Breathe ... Correctly
    Principles: *Rest, Outlook*
52. Expect Rain
    Principles: *Trust, Outlook*

FLORIDA HOSPITAL

The skill to heal. The spirit to care.®

Florida Hospital Celebration Health

Florida Hospital Altamonte

Florida Hospital Orlando

Florida Hospital Winter Park

Walt Disney Pavilion at *Florida Hospital for Children*

Florida Hospital East Orlando

Florida Hospital Apopka

Florida Hospital Kissimmee

About Florida Hospital

For over one hundred years the mission of Florida Hospital has been: *To extend the health and healing ministry of Christ.* Opened in 1908, Florida Hospital is comprised of eight hospital campuses housing over 2,200 beds and twenty walk-in medical centers. With over 17,000 employees—including 2,000 doctors and 4,000 nurses—Florida Hospital serves the residents and guests of Orlando, the No. 1 tourist destination in the world. Florida Hospital cares for over one million patients a year. Florida Hospital is a Christian, faith-based hospital that believes in providing Whole Person Care to all patients – mind, body and spirit. Hospital fast facts include:

- **LARGEST ADMITTING HOSPITAL IN AMERICA.** Ranked No. 1 in the nation for inpatient admissions by the *American Hospital Association.*

- **AMERICA'S HEART HOSPITAL.** Ranked No. 1 in the nation for number of heart procedures performed each year, averaging 15,000 cases annually. MSNBC named Florida Hospital "America's Heart Hospital" for being the No. 1 hospital fighting America's No. 1 killer—heart disease.

- **HOSPITAL OF THE FUTURE.** At the turn of the century, the *Wall Street Journal* named Florida Hospital the "Hospital of the Future."

- **ONE OF AMERICA'S BEST HOSPITALS.** Recognized by *U.S. News & World Report* as "One of America's Best Hospitals" for ten years. Clinical specialties recognized have included: Cardiology, Orthopaedics, Neurology & Neurosurgery, Urology, Gynecology, Digestive Disorders, Hormonal Disorders, Kidney Disease, Ear, Nose & Throat and Endocrinology.

- **LEADER IN SENIOR CARE.** Florida Hospital serves the largest number of seniors in America through Medicare with a goal for each patient to experience a "Century of Health" by living to a healthy hundred.

- **TOP BIRTHING CENTER.** *Fit Pregnancy* magazine named Florida Hospital one of the "Top 10 Best Places in the Country to have a Baby". As a result, *The Discovery Health Channel* struck a three-year production deal with Florida Hospital to host a live broadcast called "Birth Day Live." FH annually delivers over 8,000 babies.

- **CORPORATE ALLIANCES.** Florida Hospital maintains corporate alliance relationships with a select group of Fortune 500 companies including Disney, Nike, Johnson & Johnson, Philips, AGFA, and Stryker.

- **DISNEY PARTNERSHIP.** Florida Hospital is the Central Florida health & wellness resource of the *Walt Disney World* ® Resort. Florida Hospital also partnered with Disney to build the ground breaking health and wellness facility called Florida Hospital Celebration Health located in Disney's town of Celebration, Florida. Disney and Florida Hospital recently partnered to build a new state-of-the-art Children's Hospital.

- **HOSPITAL OF THE 21ST CENTURY.** Florida Hospital Celebration Health was awarded the *Premier Patient Services Innovator Award* as "The Model for Healthcare Delivery in the 21st Century."

Notes

Chapter 1: Turn Pretzels Into Thanksgiving Dinners

1. Jeanie Lerche Davis, "The Science of Good Deeds: The 'Helper's High' Could Help You Live a Longer, Healthier Life," WebMD, 2005, http://www.webmd.com/balance/features/science-good-deeds.
2. "Ten-Year-Old Buys Food for Two Watertown Families," NewsChannel5 .com, November 26, 2008, http://www.newschannel5.com/Global/story.asp?s=9421727.

Chapter 2: Make a Love Alphabet—For Yourself

1. The story of Misty is told in more detail in Chapter 3 of David B. Biebel, *How to Help a Heartbroken Friend*, rev. ed. (Pasadena, CA: Hope Publishing House, 2004).
2. Alfred Adler, quoted at: http://www.brainyquote.com/quotes/quotes/a/alfredadle170061.html.

Chapter 3: Go Brain Jogging

1. Lauren L. Harburger, Chinonyer K. Nzerem, and Karyn M. Frick, "Single Enrichment Variables Differentially Reduce Age-Related Memory Decline in Female Mice," *Behavioral Neuroscience* 121, no. 4 (2007): 679–88.
2. "The Right Kind of Brain Exercise Can Enhance Memory," News-Medical.Net, November 20, 2007, http://www.news-medical.net/print_article.asp?id=32684.
3. Norman Doidge, *The Brain That Changes Itself: Stories of Personal Triumph from the Frontiers of Brain Science* (New York: Penguin, 2007), 248.

Chapter 4: Count Something Other Than Beans

1. Albert Schweitzer, quoted in: http://www.brainyquote.com/quotes/quotes/a/albertschw105225.html.
2. R. A. Emmons and M. E. McCullough, "Counting blessings versus burdens: Experimental studies of gratitude and subjective well-being in daily life," *Journal of Personality and Social Psychology* 84, no. 2 (2003): 377–89.

Chapter 5: Cook Up Love in the Kitchen

1. "Organic Tomatoes Have Higher Levels of Vitamin C," News-Medical.net, July 26, 2004, http://www.news-medical.net/?id=3574.
2. Karen Asp, "Eating Healthy on a Budget," AOL Health, http://www.aolhealth.com/healthy-living/nutrition/budget-healthy-eating.

Chapter 6: Color Your World

1. Jeanette J. Fisher, "Research Concerning Color in Homes and Workplaces," *Home Improvement Information*, 2004, http://www.yourhomeinmaine.com/3383.php.

Chapter 7: Get Out of That Rut!

1. Kathleen O'Toole, "Study Takes Early Look at Social Consequences of Net Use," *Stanford University Online Report*, February 2000, http://news-service.stanford.edu/news/2000/february16/internetsurvey-216.html.
2. Dawn Kawamoto, "Survey: Many Would Take Internet over Sex,"

CNN.com, December 15, 2008, http://www.cnn.com/2008/TECH/12/15/internet.
sex.survey/index.html?iref=mpstoryview.

3. Adapted from "The Power of Spontaneity and How to Wield it," LifeDev, January 29, 2008, http://lifedev.net/2008/01/the-power-of-spontaneity-and-how-to-wield-it/.

Chapter 8: Rent a Puppy, Kitten, or Kid

1. Karen Allen, Barbara E. Shykoff, and Joseph L. Izzo, Jr., "Pet Ownership, But Not ACE Inhibitor Therapy, Blunts Home Blood Pressure Response to Mental Stress," *Hypertension* 38, no. 4 (2001): 815–20.

Chapter 9: See God's Glory in Every Place

1. Monte Swan and David Biebel, *Romancing Your Child's Heart* (Colorado Springs: Multnomah Books, 2002), 149–50.

Chapter 10: Discover Your Mode of Expression

1. "Meaningful Leisure Can Mean Many Things," News-Medical.net, June 24, 2007, http://www.news-medical.net/?id=26777.

2. Suzanne Roig, "Letting Their Artistic Impulses Fly," *Honolulu Advertiser*, August 11, 2008.

Chapter 11: Catch the Experience

1. "Testimonials," *Project Healing Waters*, 2008, http://www.projecthealingwaters.org/html/testimonials.html.

Chapter 13: Loin Cloths and Clubs Not Required

1. "Brain's 'Pleasure Chemical' Is Involved in Response to Pain Too, Study Shows," *Medical News Today*, October 21, 2006, www.medicalnewstoday.com/articles/54587.php.

2. Erma Bombeck, "Quotations about Shopping," The Quote Garden, http://www.quotegarden.com/shopping.html.

Chapter 15: Better Than an Antidepressant

1. "About The YMCA," YMCA.net, http://www.ymca.net/about_the_ymca/.

2. "Fitness Success Stories/Testimonials," http://www.greenbayymca.org/gbymca/stories/fitness+success+stories/default.asp.

3. Ibid.

Chapter 16: Delight in the Elements

1. "Australian Research Studies Health Impacts of Living in a High-rise Apartment," News-Medical.Net, September 7, 2004, http://www.news-medical.net/?id=4561.

Chapter 17: To Increase Your Energy, Test Your Skill

1. "Pure Novelty Spurs the Brain," *ScienceDaily*, August 27, 2006, http://www.sciencedaily.com/releases/2006/08/060826180547.htm.

• •

Chapter 18: Find Out Why the Pen is Mightier Than the Fog

1. James W. Pennebaker, PhD, "Writing to Heal," *The University of Texas at Austin*, March 15, 2005, http://www.utexas.edu/features/2005/writing.

Chapter 19: Spell "Surprise!" in a Whole New Way

1. K. A. Moore, PhD, S. M. Jekielek, PhD, J. Bronte-Tinkew, PhD, et al., "What Is 'Healthy Marriage'? Defining the Concept," *Child Trends Research Brief* (September 2004), http://www.acf.hhs.gov/healthymarriage/ pdf/Child_Trends-2004.pdf.

Chapter 20: Think of How Strong You're Gonna Be

1. Nalin A. Singha, Karen M. Clements, and Maria A. Fiatarone Singh, "The Efficacy of Exercise as a Long-Term Antidepressant in Elderly Subjects," *The Journals of Gerontology Series A: Biological Sciences and Medical Sciences* 56:M497-M504 (2001), http://biomed.gerontologyjournals.org/cgi/content/abstract/56/8/M497.

Chapter 21: Give Until You Feel Great

1. Jeanie Lerche Davis, "The Science of Good Deeds: The 'Helper's High' Could Help You Live a Longer, Healthier Life," *WebMD*, March 27, 2009, http://www.webmd.com/balance/features/science-good-deeds.
2. Douglas M. Lawson, PhD, *Give to Live: How Giving Can Change Your Life* (La Jolla, Calif.: ALTI Publishing, 1991), 36–37.

Chapter 22: Hit Rewind

1. Rickie Lee Jones, "Memories Quotes," http://www.stresslesscountry.com/memories-quotes/index.html.
2. Marina Krakovsky, "Nostalgia: Sweet Remembrance," *Psychology Today*, May/June 2006, http://www.psychologytoday.com/articles/pto-20060511-000003.html.
3. Ibid.

Chapter 23: Remember: You Can't Stay Mad at Someone Who Makes You Laugh

1. Dave's version of this story is based on a *Washington Post* report from "Week 228" (October 20, 1997), in which readers were asked to tell Gen-Xers how much harder they had had it in the old days. Barry Blyveis wrote, "In my day, we didn't have no rocks. We had to go down to the creek and wash our clothes by beating them with our heads." For a complete listing and some good chortling, see "The Good Old Days," *The Bad Pets List: Harold Reynolds' Humour Collection*, updated November 23, 2008, http://www.badpets.net/Humor/Lists/GoodOldDays.html.

Chapter 24: Invest Yourself

1. F. John Reh, "Mentors and Mentoring: What Is a Mentor?" About.com, http://management.about.com/cs/people/a/mentoring.htm?p=1.
2. "Mentoring," *Free Management Library*, http://www.managementhelp.org/guiding/mentrng/mentrng.htm.
3. For an extensive comparison see Joanna Lamb-White, "Coaching and Mentoring: Understanding the Differences," *TrainingZone*, May 4, 2006,

http://www.trainingzone.co.uk/cgi-bin/item.cgi?id=154289.

4. L. Rose Hollister, "Leadership in Mentoring: The Benefits of Being a Mentor," *American College of Healthcare Executives*, http://www.ache.org/newclub/CAREER/MentorArticles/Benefits.cfm.

5. Carl Mueller, "Mentoring: The Benefits of Being a Mentor," *Ezine Articles*, December 7, 2005, http://ezinearticles.com/?Mentoring:-The-Benefits-of -Being-A-Mentor&id=109135.

Chapter 26: Put on Your Own Mask First

1. Laura Schiff and Hollis Kline, "Water's Wonders," *Psychology Today*, Sept./Oct. 2001, http://www.psychologytoday.com/articles/pto-20010901-000032.html.

Chapter 28: Seek Buried Treasure

1. This story is based on and excerpted from *Romancing Your Child's Heart* by Monte Swan and David Biebel (Colorado Springs: Multnomah Books), 228–30. It is reproduced more completely in *The Secret of Singing Springs* (Orlando, FL: Healthy Life Press, 2012).

Chapter 29: Play for Your Own Enjoyment and Amazement

1. Duane Shinn, "Piano Lessons for Adults," Best-interview-strategies.com, http://www.best-interview-strategies.com/article62.html.

2. Bob Karlovits, "Adults Take Music Lessons for a Variety of Reasons," *Pittsburgh Tribune-Review*, March 14, 2006, http://www.pittsburghlive.com/x/pittsburghtrib/s_433027.html.

3. "Every Life Is Better with Music: The Benefits Are Better Than You Think," *American Music Conference*, 2007, http://www.amcmusic.com/school_age_social.htm.

4. "Mission and Vision," *Opus 118 Harlem School of Music*, http://www.opus118.org/.

5. "Seniors: Music Impacts Learning, Health and Wellness," *American Music Conference*, 2007, http://www.amc-music.com/seniors_social.htm.

6. "Bringing Music to Life: Discovering What It Has to Offer," *American Music Conference*, 2007, http://www.amc-music.com/musicmaking/what_instrument.htm.

Chapter 30: Try the Nonfattening, Noninvasive, Performance-Enhancing, Mood-Lifter

1. "Siestas Good for Your Heart," *News-Medical.net*, February 12, 2007, www.news-medical.net/?id=21842.

Chapter 31: Acknowledge Your Need to Be Kneaded

1. "The Power of Touch for Pain Relief: Basic Facts," *The American Massage Therapy Association*, October 2003, http://www.amtamassage.org/news/painfactsheet.html.

Chapter 32: Be the Bear

1. Matina Horner introduced this theory in her PhD dissertation. For her biography, see http://www.bookrags.com/biography/matina-souretis-horner/.
2. For a technical overview of continuing analysis of Horner's theory, see Ralph L. Piedmont, "Another Look at Fear of Success, Fear of Failure, and Test Anxiety: A Motivational Analysis Using the Five-Factor Model," *Sex Roles: A Journal of Research* (Feb. 1995), available online at http://findarticles.com/p/articles/mi_m2294/is_n34_v32/ai_17212886/pg_1?tag=artBody;col1.
3. This quote is from David B. Biebel and Howard Lawrence, eds., *Pastors Are People Too* (Ventura, CA: Regal Books, 1986), 161. This book is now out of print, but a few copies are available from Dr. Biebel, who can be reached by e-mail at DBBV1@aol.com.
4. Marianne Williamson, *A Return to Love: Reflections on the Principles of a Course in Miracles* (New York: HarperCollins, 1992), 165.

Chapter 33: Get Off the Gerbil Wheel

1. "Voluntary Simplicity: Living and Having More With Less," *Great River Earth Institute*, http://www.greatriv.org/vs.htm.
2. "Cut the Stress, Simplify Your Life," *WebMD*, August 25, 2008, http://www.webmd.com/balance/guide/cut-stress-simplify-life.
3. Ibid.
4. Lisa McLaughlin, "How to Live with Just 100 Things," *Time*, June 5, 2008, http://www.time.com/time/magazine/article/0,9171,1812048,00.html.
5. Ellen Michaud with Julie Bain, "Five Proven Ways to Simplify Your Life," *Reader's Digest*, 2008, http://www.rd.com/living-healthy/5-proven-strategies-to-simplify-your-life-for-deeper-sleep/article54369.html.
6. Ibid.

Chapter 34: Put Tele-Working to Work

1. Mark J. Penn with E. Kinney Zalesne, *Microtrends* (New York: Hachette Book Group, 2007), 39–42.
2. "Telecommuting," Columbia Encyclopedia article on AOL Search Reference Center, http://plus.aol.com/aol/reference/telecommut/telecommuting?flv=1.
3. Richard Russell, "The Perfect Business," *Richard Russell's Dow Theory Letters Online*, http://ww2.dowtheoryletters.com/DTLOL.nsf/htmlmedia/body_the_perfect_business.html.
4. If you would like our help researching your options, contact authors.

Chapter 36: Become Not Like the Tin Man

1. Ian Shrier, MD, PhD, and Kav Gossal, MD, "Myths and Truths of Stretching," *The Physician and Sportsmedicine* 28, no. 8 (August 2000).

Chapter 37: Stop Fixin' to Do Something

1. Kathleen McGowan, "Is the To-Do List Doing You In?" *Psychology Today*, December 2005, http://www.psychologytoday.com/articles/pto-20051207-000001.html.

2. Ibid.
3. Hara Estroff Marano, "Are You a Procrastinator?" *Psychology Today*, July 2005, http://www.psychologytoday.com/articles/pto-20050727-00007.html.
4. McGowan, "Is the To-Do List Doing You In?"

Chapter 38: Unearth Those Skeletons

1. "Genealogy," *Wikipedia.org*, updated March 27, 2009, http://en.wikipedia .org/wiki/Genealogy.
2. Allison Merline, "Genealogy Benefits," *Ezine Articles*, April 18, 2008, http://ezinearticles.com/?Genealogy-Benefits&id=1119496.
3. Alyson Kenward, "Genealogy: The Secrets Behind a Serious Leisure Activity," *University of Calgary*, 2003, http://www.ucalgary.ca/mp2003/unicomm/research/stories/genealogy.html.
4. Ibid.
5. Lester J. Hartrick, "The Psychological Benefits of Genealogy," RootsWeb at Ancestry.com, December 28, 2000, http://freepages.genealogy. rootsweb.ancestry.com/~hartrickclan/article5.htm.

Chapter 39: Rock On, Groove to the Beat, or Hum with a Hymn

1. For information about Young at Heart, see http://www.foxsearchlight.com/youngatheart/.
2. Roger H. Meyer, "The Sounds of Music: Music Can Have Remarkable Benefits for Your Health, Or It Can Be Destructive," *Vibrant Life*, Nov.-Dec. 2003, available online at http://findarticles.com/p/articles/mi_m0826/is_6_19/ai_111111453.
3. Ibid.
4. "Elevator Music," *Wikipedia.org*, updated March 25, 2009, http://en.wikipedia.org/wiki/Elevator_music.
5. Mike Seddon, "Can Listening to Music Help Us Work Better?" *Articlesbase.com*, October 30, 2006, http://www.articlesbase.com/self-help-articles/can-listening-to-music-help-us-work-better-68598.html.
6. Scotie Keithlow, "Listening to Soothing Music Is a Great Way to Relax," *Ezine Articles*, March 16, 2008, http://ezinearticles.com/?Listening-To -Soothing-Music-Is-A-Great-Way-To-Relax!&id=1049078.
7. Anna Lynn C. Sibal, "Healing Music," *BeautyDen.com*, http://www.beautyden.com/healingmusic.shtml.

Chapter 40: Hang Ten!

1. Sian Beilock et al., "Sports Experience Enhances the Neural Processing of Action Language," *Proceedings of the National Academy of Sciences*, September 1, 2008, http://www.physorg.com/news139508489.html.
2. "How Great Thou Art," by Carl Gustav Boberg, 1885.

Chapter 41: Try a "Spice to Life" Meal

1. "Food Like an Addictive Drug for Some People," *News-Medical.net*, October 3, 2006, http://www.news-medical.net/?id=20366.

Chapter 42: Tune to the Maker's Channel
1. Henri J. M. Nouwen, *The Way of the Heart* (San Francisco: Harper & Row, 1981), 43.
2. Used by permission from Dr. Michael P. Brooks, Christian Outdoor Fellowship of America. For information see http://www.cofausa.org.

Chapter 43: Set Sail for New Adventures
1. "Reading on the Rise: A New Chapter in American Literacy," http://www.nea.gov/research/ReadingonRise.pdf.
2. "Ten Benefits of Reading," *I News India*, September 29, 2008, http://www.inewsindia.com/2008/09/29/10-benefits-of-reading/.

Chapter 44: Go Surfing With No Board
1. "Blog," *Wikipedia*, updated 4/3/2009, http://en.wikipedia.org/wiki/Blog.
2. "Paul Potts' First Audition," Britain's Got Talent, YouTube.com, June 16, 2007, http://www.youtube.com/watch?v=sxOytYLlhiQ.

Chapter 46: Follow Your Nose
1. Cheryl A. Sweet, "Scents and Nonsense: Does Aromatherapy Stink?" *American Council on Science and Health* (Oct. 1997). (accessed 9/12/2011).
2. "Aromatherapy May Make You Feel Good, But It Won't Make You Well" *Research News, Ohio State University*. http://researchnews.osu.edu/archive/aromatherapy.htm. (accessed 9/12/2011).
3. H. Kuriyama, S. Watanabe,T. Nakaya, et al. "Immunilogical and Psychological Benefits of Aromatherapy Massage," *Evidence Based Complement Alternative Med.* (June 2(2) 2005 Jun;2(2):179-184. Epub.
4. "The Benefits of Aromatherapy: M.D. Anderson Teaches How To Soothe and Heal." www.medicalnewstoday.com/releases/50591.php. Aug 29, 2006. (accessed 9/12/2011).
5. "Aromatherapy." University of Maryland Medical Center web site at www.umm.edu/altmed/articles-000347.htm (accessed 9/12/2011).

Chapter 47: Keep Company With "My Left Foot"
1. "AFI's 100 Years . . . 100 Cheers," American Film Institute. See: http://www.infoplease.com/ipea/A0934314.html. (Accessed Nov. 5, 2011).
2. "Most Inspirational Movies of All Time," MovieFone. See: http://www.moviefone.com/insidemovies/2008/11/03/best-inspirtional-movies/?icid=200100397x1212609074x1200833162. (Accessed Nov. 5, 2011).

Chapter 48: Unfold Your Family Life
1. "Scrapbooking," *Wikipedia*, updated March 25, 2009, http://en.wikipedia.org/wiki/Scrapbook.
2. For information about "Memories That Matter" scrapbooking retreats at Singing Hills Christian Conference Center in New Hampshire, call toll-free 1-888-863-2267.

Chapter 50: Take Up the First Occupation

1. Larisa Brass, "Seed Seller Says Sales Are Booming as More People Plant Gardens," *Knoxville News Sentinel*, May 31, 2008, http://www.knoxnews.com/news/2008/may/31/seed-seller-says-sales-are-booming-more-people-pla/.
2. Sandra Mason, "Health Benefits of Gardening," *University of Illinois Extension Homeowner's Column*, January 3, 2005, http://web.extension.uiuc.edu/champaign/homeowners/050103.html.
3. Ibid.

Chapter 51: Just Breathe . . . Correctly

1. "Breathing—the Proper Technique." http://www.stop-anxiety-attack-symptoms.com/breathing.html.
2. Ibid.
3. Ibid.
4. Marcelle Pick. "Deep Breathing—the Truly Essential Exercise." http://www.womentowomen.com/fatigueandstress/deepbreathing.aspx. (Accessed Nov. 5, 2011).
5. Ibid.
6. "Research on Deep Breathing May Bring Relief to Asthmatics." http://www.medscape.com/viewarticle/412082. (Accessed Nov. 5, 2011).

Chapter 52: Expect Rain

1. David Biebel, *If God Is So Good, Why Do I Hurt So Bad?* (Orlando, FL: Healthy Life Press, 2010), 142.

LEAD YOUR COMMUNITY
TO HEALTHY
LIVING

With C·R·E·A·T·I·O·N Health Seminars, Books, & Resources

SHOP OUR ONLINE STORE AT:

CREATIONhealth.com

FOR MANY MORE RESOURCES

> "CREATION Health has made a tremendous impact as part of the health ministries of our church and has also changed my life! We plan to continue an ongoing CREATION Health seminar at Forest Lake Church."
>
> ~ Derek Morris, Senior Pastor, Forest Lake Church

SEMINAR MATERIALS

Leader Guide
Everything a leader needs to conduct this seminar successfully, including key questions to facilitate group discussion and PowerPoint presentations for each of the eight principles.

Participant Guide
A study guide with essential information from each of the eight lessons along with outlines, self assessments, and questions for people to fill-in as they follow along.

Small Group Kit
It's easy to lead a small group using the CREATION Health videos, the Small Group Leaders Guide and the Small Group Discussion Guide.

Healthy 100 Resources

8 Secrets of a Healthy 100 (Softcover)

Can you imagine living to a Healthy 100 years of age? Dr. Des Cummings Jr., explores the principles practiced by the All-stars of Longevity to live longer and more abundantly. Take a journey through the 8 Secrets and you will be inspired to imagine living to a Healthy 100.

CREATION Health Discovery (Softcover)

CREATION Health Discovery takes the 8 essential principles of CREATION Health and melds them together to form the blueprint for the health we yearn for and the life we are intended to live.

CREATION Health Breakthrough (Hardcover)

Blending science and lifestyle recommendations, Monica Reed, MD, prescribes eight essentials that will help reverse harmful health habits and prevent disease. Discover how intentional choices, rest, environment, activity, trust, relationships, outlook, and nutrition can put a person on the road to wellness. Features a three-day total body rejuvenation therapy and four-phase life transformation plan.

CREATION Health Devotional (English) (Hardcover)

Stories change lives. Stories can inspire health and healing. In this devotional you will discover stories about experiencing God's grace in the tough times, God's delight in triumphant times, and God's presence in peaceful times. Based on the eight timeless principles of wellness: Choice, Rest, Environment, Activity, Trust, Interpersonal relationships, Outlook, Nutrition.

CREATION Health Devotional (Spanish) (Softcover)

CREATION Health Devotional for Women (English)

Written for women by women, the CREATION Health Devotional for Women is based on the principles of whole-person wellness represented in CREATION Health. Spirits will be lifted and lives rejuvenated by the message of each unique chapter. This book is ideal for women's prayer groups, to give as a gift, or just to buy for your own edification and encouragement.

Healthy 100 Resources

Forgive To Live *(English) (Hardcover)*

In *Forgive to Live* Dr. Tibbits presents the scientifically proven steps for forgiveness – taken from the first clinical study of its kind conducted by Stanford University and Florida Hospital.

Forgive To Live *(Spanish) (Softcover)*

Forgive To Live Workbook *(Softcover)*

This interactive guide will show you how to forgive – insight by insight, step by step – in a workable plan that can effectively reduce your anger, improve your health, and put you in charge of your life again, no matter how deep your hurts.

Forgive To Live Devotional *(Hardcover)*

In his powerful new devotional Dr. Dick Tibbits reveals the secret to forgiveness. This compassionate devotional is a stirring look at the true meaning of forgiveness. Each of the 56 spiritual insights includes motivational Scripture, an inspirational prayer, and two thought-provoking questions. The insights are designed to encourage your journey as you begin to *Forgive to Live*.

Forgive To Live God's Way *(Softcover)*

Forgiveness is so important that our very lives depend on it. Churches teach us that we should forgive, but how do you actually learn to forgive? In this spiritual workbook noted author, psychologist, and ordained minister Dr. Dick Tibbits takes you step-by-step through an eight-week forgiveness format that is easy to understand and follow.

Forgive To Live Leader's Guide

Perfect for your community, church, small group or other settings.

The *Forgive to Live Leader's Guide* Includes:

- 8 Weeks of pre-designed PowerPoint™ presentations.
- Professionally designed customizable marketing materials and group handouts on CD-Rom.
- Training directly from author of *Forgive to Live* Dr. Dick Tibbits across 6 audio CDs.
- Media coverage DVD.
- CD-Rom containing all files in digital format for easy home or professional printing.
- A copy of the first study of its kind conducted by Stanford University and Florida Hospital showing a link between decreased blood pressure and forgiveness.
- Much more!

Healthy 100 Resources

If Today Is All I Have *(Softcover)*

At its heart, Linda's captivating account chronicles the struggle to reconcile her three dreams of experiencing life as a "normal woman" with the tough realities of her medical condition. Her journey is punctuated with insights that are at times humorous, painful, provocative, and life-affirming.

Pain Free For Life *(Hardcover)*

In *Pain Free For Life*, Scott C. Brady, MD, – founder of Florida Hospital's Brady Institute for Health – shares for the first time with the general public his dramatically successful solution for chronic back pain, Fibromyalgia, chronic headaches, Irritable bowel syndrome and other "impossible to cure" pains. Dr. Brady leads pain-racked readers to a pain-free life using powerful mind-body-spirit strategies used at the Brady Institute – where more than 80 percent of his chronic-pain patients have achieved 80-100 percent pain relief within weeks.

Original Love *(Softcover)*

Are you ready for: God's smile to affirm your worth? God's forgiveness to renew your relationship? God's courage to calm your fears? God's gifts to fulfill your dreams? The God who made you is ready to give you all this and so much more! Join Des Cummings Jr., PhD, as he unfolds God's love drama in the life stories of Old Testament heroes. He provides fresh, biblical light on the original day God made for love. His wife, Mary Lou, shares practical, creative ways to experience Sabbath peace, blessings, and joy!

SuperSized Kids *(Hardcover)*

In *SuperSized Kids*, Walt Larimore, MD, and Sherri Flynt, MPH, RD, LD, show how the mushrooming childhood obesity epidemic is destroying children's lives, draining family resources, and pushing America dangerously close to a total healthcare collapse – while also explaining, step by step, how parents can work to avert the coming crisis by taking control of the weight challenges facing every member of their family.

SuperFit Family Challenge - Leader's Guide

Perfect for your community, church, small group or other settings.

The *SuperFit Family Challenge Leader's Guide* Includes:

- 8 Weeks of pre-designed PowerPoint™ presentations.
- Professionally designed marketing materials and group handouts from direct mailers to reading guides.
- Training directly from Author Sherri Flynt, MPH, RD, LD, across 6 audio CDs.
- Media coverage and FAQ on DVD.
- Much more!

www.FloridaHospitalPublishing.com

www.Facebook.com/FloridaHospitalPublishing

IMAGINE...

A body that is healthy and strong,

A spirit that is vibrant and refreshed,

A life that glorifies God,

Imagine living to a Healthy 100!

What is the Healthy 100 Church Association?

The goal of the Healthy 100 movement is simple: inspire individuals, families and communities to fill their days with God's power, passion and purpose, enabling them to live long and vibrant lives.

The Healthy 100 Church Association inspires, informs and equips churches, pastors, faith community nurses, health ministers and lay leaders to transform people through principles of whole-person health and healing. Our vision for the Healthy 100 Church Association is to partner with you while providing a health and healing platform full of incredible inspiration and practical implementation resources. This life-enhancing outreach of health ministry can help your church create a place where God's people live abundant lives full of physical, mental and spiritual health. After all, Jesus said: *"I have come that they may have life, and have it to the full."* John 10:10

In this association, you will:

▶ **Be Inspired** - Connect and participate in a thriving online community only for Healthy 100 churches where you can share ideas, resources and prayer requests.

▶ **Be Informed** – Continue the journey of learning about faith and health connections with online health ministry training on how to start a vibrant health ministry in your congregation, monthly webinars and active blogs.

▶ **Be Equipped** – Access the vibrant Healthy 100 Church Association database with hundreds of health and healing implementation resources, such as videos, bulletin excerpts, lunch 'n learns, tools and surveys, awareness campaigns and much more that will help you engage your congregation to be at their best for serving God. You will also receive a 20 percent discount on Healthy 100 resources, including books, small-group materials, seminar materials and the annual *Imagine a Healthy 100 | Church Simulcast.*

Become a Healthy 100 church by visiting www.Healthy100Churches.org

FLORIDA HOSPITAL

Healthy100Churches.org

H100CHUR-11-4773